Passing the Baton

Reginald Ryder

i

Table of Contents

Dedication & Acknowledgments

I want to first thank God for my life and the gifts He has entrusted me with using. I have not always known what they were, and now that I am aware of them, I plan to continue to use it for the greater good and His glory.

Marvin and Joyce Ryder, Dad and Mom, this book is dedicated to your hard work and many unrealized sacrifices. You supplied the discipline, lessons, and affirmations I applied in my own life. I have fully bloomed. You did not let your circumstances hold you down or allow it to be used as an excuse. Those principles were instilled in me, and I am all the better for it. Your voice is forever in my head, "Be the best at whatever you do!" Thank you!

Thank you to my wife, the mother of my kids, my best friend and "ride or die" partner, Kim Amaker Ryder. When I at times have hit a wall, you told me to climb over it and make a way. When a man finds a wife, he finds a good thing and receives favor from God. Well, I hope favor will continue to flow as bountifully as it has. I am rich. You are my soulmate and will be forever more. I love you.

To my children, Kristina Noel and Reginald David II, I know you are on lease to your mother and I. I love you both so much and want nothing more than the best for you. You are amazing in your own right and I hope the lessons I have instilled will continue to shape you now and for the rest of your life. I will always have your back.

To my siblings Randy, Gwen, Ron and Regina, thank you for your undying support as your baby brother. I have learned many lessons and have had some great times with you all. We have a special relationship and an unusual bond that has kept us close. I truly love and appreciate you.

For my in-laws and extended family, Deborah Amaker, Raymond Amaker, Patricia McLean, Bob Wilson, Karen Amaker, Krystal Amaker, Kamara Amaker, Brian Amaker, Maya Amaker, Justin Amaker, and Kara Ryder, thank you so much for our connection and I hope I have nurtured you as much as you have nurtured me. Also, to my nieces and nephews, I love you.

A special thank you to the thousands of students that I have encountered and attempted to make a difference in the lives of. I hope I contributed to your life in a way that continues to shape your day to day. Some of your stories of trial and success live here and continue to shape many lives.

A special thanks to the many K-12 educators, student affairs administrators, and professionals that I have worked with day to day or who mentored me in the various roles that I have served in. It has made all the difference and brought my gifts to life.

For the many well-wishers who have inspired me to write this book, I could not have done it without your support. Thanks Dr. Jonathan Townsend, Rebecca Robinson, Sara Seiberling, Candace and Everette Kenyatta, Jonathan (Pitty) and Rachel Pittman, Petiecha Cummings Reese, Suraju Jolaoso,

Vanessa Solomon, Pastor Tony Lewis, First Lady Charlet Lewis, Dr. Mario McCoy, Alyssa Cole, Stacey Jacobs, Ron Collins, Derrick and Ramunda Young, Dr. Lewita Shatee, Petra Gomez, Keeon and Traci Gregory, and TC Johnson for believing in me when I did not see this endeavor for myself.

My editor and friend, Erica Collins, thank you so much for making sense of my thoughts and story. The critique was objective and gentle. I did not know what to anticipate with this part of the process, and you surpassed my expectations with your level of professionalism. Ironically, you and I have come full circle now from me assisting you through USC and now you as my editor. I hope we can continue this cycle many times over.

Dr. SyLinda Musaindapo, "Dr. Sy," I appreciate you from our initial conversations at 2U that we had about my attempt to move forward with a business idea and the tips you offered. Our passion for First-Generation students, higher education, retention, and coaching has been so aligned that it only made sense for you to write the Foreword for this book. I have great respect for you and am so honored by the role you have played in this process.

First Lady Charlet Lewis, thank you for planting the seed of writing this book last May. I did not see it immediately, yet once I did, I could not stop writing until I got to the end. Here is the fruit of my labor from the seed you planted. Thank you for your help with publishing this book. It has been immensely helpful. I could not have done it without you.

Since this past July, all of you have played a key role in the development of this book and I could not have done it without you. Thank you! Your candor and direction have helped me immensely. If I omitted your name and you played a part in this process with me, accept my apology.

I love and appreciate all of you in my circle.

Sincerely,

Reginald David Ryder, M.Ed.

Founder, Thriving Life Coaching

Foreword

Four years ago, I was visiting the Washington, D.C. area on a business trip. I worked for an educational technology company that partners with colleges and universities to host their degree programs online through a hands-on and engaging partnership. At the time, I served as a Student Success Advisor for MBA students. I worked from the company's Denver office, and visited the Maryland location to connect with my colleagues face-to-face. On a lunch break, I was eager to meet with the author of this book, Reginald Ryder. I had been energized by his passion and intention for student success through previous online meetings and interactions. His positive and encouraging demeanor made me excited to explore how we could help each other expand our circle of influence in the education field. Like me, Reginald understood the challenges and victories associated with succeeding as a first-generation college student. We shared a passion for wanting to give students encouragement, support and pragmatic resources that would support their higher education journeys. During that lunch meeting, we dreamed and brainstormed together. Reginald's passion made it clear that he was onto something special-- he was about to change his corner of the world!

Education is my calling. My career has been centered around education in various capacities. As a teenager, I fell in love with education after taking a "Teaching Teachers How to

Teach" course at my church. I earned an academic scholarship to major in elementary education at a prestigious university, and I had no idea what I was getting myself into! I knew very little about what to expect as a college student. I was not prepared to gather the documentation that was necessary to complete my financial aid application. I knew that my scholarship covered tuition, but I was not prepared to pay $500/semester for textbooks. I was not emotionally prepared to face racism from my professors and classmates. I almost lost my voice until I engaged with a community that strengthened me, motivated me, and encouraged me to overcome. I went on to transfer to another institution where I felt I belonged. After completing my bachelor's degree in English, I worked in community-based healthcare education and taught middle school for three years. I later returned to earn my masters and doctoral degrees in Adult and Higher Education. I have taught on college and university campuses and served as a leader for retention and student success. I am an expert in first-year experience best practices. I currently assist graduate-level faculty maximize their skills and resources while they teach online. Additionally, I serve as a life coach and mentor for people in transitional places in life. I share my story for this reason: I have read dozens of books that are designed to help students as they transition into college. This is one of the most timeless and relevant books about college success.

As I read this book, I was filled with the same energy and passion that I experienced during our first lunch meeting. Reginald and I have continued to work alongside each other through Student Success and global diversity efforts. We both chair our respective office's Black Engagement Network. He is not just an expert though! Reginald serves as a professor and mentor in the local community. This book is filled with practical wisdom from a person who knows what he's talking about and *cares about you!* You can read this book from cover to cover or use it as a reference guide that you refer to throughout your collegiate career. It is filled with relatable stories that will empower you to be successful. I will warn you: he keeps it real! You will not be able to read this book and not be empowered to take authority over your educational experience.

Parents, caretakers, practitioners and faculty can use this as a manual for first year-experience courses or a resource for mentoring and supporting college students. I am both honored and excited to witness the development of an organization and college student manual that will change lives and improve the college experience for other first-generation students or individuals looking to improve their academic status and reach their full potential. Congratulations on starting your journey! The fact that you chose this book means your off to a strong start!

Dr. SyLinda Musaindapo, Ed. D.

Chapter 1

Square One
College Material

The journey of one thousand miles for a college student begins with the first step. Take Nina for example. She is a 17-year-old nearing her 18th birthday and has just graduated from high school. As she feasts her eyes on the reflection of her accomplishment, a great sigh of relief and joy overcome her. She sees the flashbulbs of the camera spark the air, capturing the image of a smile and handshake from a school official handing her the high school diploma that she just earned. Nina hears the screams when her full name is announced to the crowded auditorium full of families, friends, and well-wishers. As she returns to her seat with the diploma clutched in her hands, many thoughts enter her head. The most prominent one being that she will be the first among her siblings to go to college.

A few days later after graduation was over, I wanted to connect with Nina to congratulate her. As Nina sits for our coaching session, this is among many thoughts still weighing heavy on her mind. Nina and I went to our usual spot, the quaint little coffee shop on the corner of McKinley and Port Republic. We always sit at the back corner away from the hustle and bustle of the counter and the door swinging back and forth. Her demeanor was a little different today and I wanted to know what was on her mind. I listened to her mull over her decision to attend college and the preparation for her next steps. She held her Latte' filled cup and said:

"College! The next challenge on my list of goals in preparation for the rest of my life. To this point, I have been able to rise to the occasion and have something to show for it. The journey to this point has been made up of highs and lows, triumphs and trials. I have worked hard and tirelessly to get here. I have arrived at this pivotal crossroad with the help and support of many or at times only a few. My parents, you, teachers, mentors, and many others have offered kernels of wisdom. Even the individuals that for whatever unknown reason offered me commentary like, 'I am not sure college is right for you', or 'This school seems like a reach for you. Are you sure about this?' It may have inspired me to prove them wrong or to confirm in my own mind that I am "college material" and not suffering from "imposter syndrome" (defined as a mind-set that an individual is doubting that they really belong in a specific situation or status despite the fact that they have accomplishments illustrating their capability and competency). The drive and commitment to embrace this specific moment puts me in a special position. I may be the first in my family tree that lays down the foundation that others will follow. Generations from now, people will look at this moment and see this as the spark that started a long tradition of college students after me. I want to be able to shape my future with the work ethic laid down by many before me. I want to just do this my way, the best I can. Set the bar high, laying the foundation for many to come behind me – yes, even at my young age, a legacy under construction."

With a sigh of relief from her monologue and with the enormity of her new opportunity, Nina's pause was deliberate as she looked me square in the eye, "Now, what do I do to make this college experience mean something in a brand new and unknown environment?"

My Gift

In the following pages you will learn the answers to her question, "How do I master this next phase of my life?" This guide's purpose is to offer a pragmatic and easily constructed path to understand how to master the process of successfully completing your college experience with more confidence than chaos. If you are reading this book in middle school or high school, you will be paving a path that should make the process manageable. I am divulging the behind the scenes efforts it will take for you to maximize your skills and talents in tangible ways that begin the process of you being a life-long learner. It has been tested twice, as a student in my own experience and as a practitioner assisting students through the college excursion. There is no secret formula or magic wand. It's old school hard work used under the right conditions that you set which will allow this to work for you.

Applying these skills will not only help you with college, it will allow you to thrive in a globally competitive workplace. I have chosen to offer not only a template for your success, but also use my mistakes and milestones to mark each leg of the journey. It will also be seen through the prism of former students and their experiences, both good and bad. If you are willing to run this race with me and use the nuggets of wisdom properly, "the baton" I possess will soon be yours to offer beyond the construct of this book and be a living breathing gift. A gift that will shape the lives of many who are open to its message.

The Apprentice

Regardless of how you have arrived at this point, college is a blank slate awaiting your tools to carve a great masterpiece, your life. Your time has arrived, but how did you get here? The process of attending the many college fairs far and wide, the high school visits from college admissions reps, and school workshops on the application process or financial aid seminars have ended. You have now transitioned to the college visits to your schools you applied to and the many visits to the campus bookstore to collect all the latest gear during campus tours, reviewing all the acceptance letters and maybe a rejection or waitlist notification, and the final visits to the short list of schools just to confirm your commitment and assurance of the best or final decision before deposit deadlines. With your final decision locked in, you are attending orientation with your family to meet many of your fellow classmates, advisors, and university personnel that will affect the next "best four or five years of your life."

Yes. That statement is true, but do not forget the fine print all the way at the bottom of the page. These are the best years. College is probably one of the greatest times to explore and emerge as a more informed person - a life-long learner. Your parents, although connected to you, are likely miles or hours away. While the time or distance is not as much a part of this, you are now on your own maybe for the very first time in your life. Their safety net is close enough for you to fall into - provided you decide to use it. You have an ability to brand or even rebrand yourself. You can figure out what you like, what you are truly passionate about, and you are willing to explore all the possibilities to make it become a reality. This is a time for you to learn from your mistakes. Yes, believe it or not, you will make mistakes. Do so, so that you learn the lesson from them and apply them to your life. Now some mistakes you cannot recover from; however, there are some mistakes that force you to evaluate and adjust properly to make more informed choices. Opportunities like this must be taken advantage of to gain the full experience. Speaking of which, this is the time to try new things that maybe you were not sure about previously. This is not limited to food. You will connect with the people at college in so many ways whether they are mentors, classmates, roommates, fraternity or sorority members, clubs, or sports teammates. Making some sacrifices and being committed to this from start to finish will establish a clear path towards your success. At this point in your life, you have minimal obligations, few or no bills, might be single, and don't have another person's considerations to factor into your major decisions. In most cases, you have a pretty clear view of the world and how you would like it to run. This newfound freedom means you get to make every choice along the way. This also means that you are completely responsible for the outcomes and consequences that come your way as well. The autonomy, independence, and freedom offered entrusts that you will do the right thing as often as possible, making the best choice. Best choice does not always mean what fulfills your immediate need. It is the choice that is going to be the most beneficial to your future. How will each decision impact the next one you need to make? Will it take you two steps forward, or two steps backwards? Therefore, this next stanza of your life is among the best time. It is an exploration that prepares you in many ways for adulthood.

Chapter 2

My Legacy Under Construction

These lessons and preparation for this big step are now so apparent to me as a seasoned professional in higher education. However, as a first-generation student (parents did not attend college or attain a degree), I had no blueprint to build upon. I had to start from scratch. As much as my parents wanted this opportunity for me, we did not have any point of reference for me to draw on in my preparation. I knew the outcome I wanted was to attain a college degree, but I had no concept of the process.

Application Process

Looking back on it now, I do not remember much of the college application process. Mostly because there was not much of one. It was not as involved and elaborate of a process as it is now for your generation. The amount of resources available to you now in some ways make it easier to engage. I remember going to my guidance office at my high school and picked up one paper application from Ms. Zumbrun to Ball State University. There was no conversation about what to expect or wise counsel offered. I offer this not as a fault of anyone, just my reality at the time. I knew of BSU from hearing other kids who talked about it and their appearance in the NCAA Basketball Tournament the year before. I filled out the application in pen, crushing my handwritten responses in the small spaces offered after each question and waited for their decision of my acceptance. One school, one decision. I remember one night in the fall of my senior year getting a call from a BSU student ambassador on the phone. The call was to check in with me to see if I had any questions about anything related to the school, and as an uninformed and unprepared 17-year-old, I offered a simple response – "no," and hung up the phone. I did not know what I did not know. My older brothers had gone to the US Air Force and college at another state school. My older sister was commuting to a local community college, and my twin sister was being recruited to run track, but no school was offering a home visit or athletic scholarship. Asking them would have been fine, but we were all in the same boat. Again, I was naïve and ignorant to the process. That's why when I eventually worked in Admissions at Ball State University, Butler University, and Cornell University, I took the opportunity to really explain the college process to prospective parents and students. I remembered that uninformed student years back who did not know what to ask when given the opportunity. I wanted to create a new experience so that my situation would not be repeated in these students' lives.

Working with What You Have

The dilemma I faced was not having immediate resources in place to get the answers I needed. I was not savvy to this specific situation and had no concept of what it meant being ready for college. You see by no fault of their own, my mother and father were born during the Great Depression in the Jim

Crow South of Georgia. A black person's place in this segregated, derogated, violent, and turbulent setting was a refilled prescription written and duplicated over and over again. You did not have one! Unfortunately, you are at the mercy or menacing practices which illustrated your perpetual lack of worth in the South and many places in the country. Thus, their access to basic education was minimal, substandard and unequal at best with financial resources meant for survival rather than a college fund. My mother was fortunate. From a working-class family, she graduated from high school and worked for some time at a local department store for meager wages. Neither of her parents went to college. My father had a similar situation. Neither of his parents went to college and gained only a middle school education. In either case, it did not mean they were not smart, just not formally trained and minimal access to aspire to a college education. During my dad's 10th grade year in high school, it was necessary for him to quit. He worked to help support his family for a time, moving on his own and then joined the US Air Force. While in the US Air Force, he received his GED and took some community college courses as well as lots of training opportunities over his 27-year career. At times, early on in his career he spent time reading the dictionary and extra books to catch up to his peers. The USAF became his "college" and as he excelled, it led to a decorated career being a leader of men and women in uniform. A job well done considering his meager start and initial social status in America.

This world of college was not completely foreign to me, but I definitely did not know it like the back of my hand either. I lacked relevant first-hand knowledge of going away and hitting the books. It seemed so easy and glamorized as I watched in movies and television shows. There was obviously so much more to it than I had imagined.

9

The Envelope Please

I remember getting my letter of acceptance to the only school that I applied to. With no plan B, it was where I was going to go to school; now came the scramble for financial aid for grants and loans. "Yes! A substantial enough of a package so I could go, Whew!" After my acceptance of the aid and the deposit being sent, I attended the orientation by myself because my parents were working. My twin sister and I ended up attending the same university. Being a military family, I by no means was sheltered in my exposure of the world. I had lived in South Dakota, Georgia, Oregon and Indiana. By the age of ten, I became accustomed to living on military installations and attending different schools. Access to what life had to offer was good and I had transitioned well in varying environments. Also, I was athletic and outgoing, so this part I knew.

From Foreign to Familiar Territory

College was going to be a totally different experience and I had no point of reference. I knew school was important, but I had no idea how it would impact every portion of my life. If I knew then what I know now, I would have not wasted so much time in figuring it out. I would have done it from the beginning in middle school or high school. My evolution from a naive young man and novice to a college environment to directing and guiding students through this process now is not what I imagined or predicted and is even still amazing to me. The various roles I have served recruiting students and helping them complete their academic work in preparation for their life has been rewarding and fulfilling. It has been amazing to work in the field of higher education and gain all of this valuable experience, passion, diligence, and information there is out there and now be able to offer it back to you in the many forums I have worked over my 30 years. This book is an opportunity to distill for you my own experiences as well as my observations of the thousands of students I have worked with, revealing our triumphs, trials, challenges, and successes in a space to help you become a better student.

Purpose and Pedigree

This book is my attempt to even your playing field and offer knowledge that I did not have then and have acquired after years of experience. I am offering you what I practiced as a student and what I developed as a professional specializing in student retention. I wanted to bring this to your attention, so minimally you plant the kernels of wisdom you need so they grow and mature in fertile soil bearing the kind of fruit you are capable of producing. As a current life coach, adjunct faculty member, student success advisor, and previously admissions representative, multicultural affairs director, director of guidance, assistant dean of students, student, spouse, and parent, I have worked with thousands of students in private schools, prestigious postsecondary institutions and now digital education. The forum has changed, but the operation remains the same; prepare yourself.

Chapter 3

Lesson 1:
YOU ARE THE CLIENT!?

At the very core of your experience, you should know that you are an integral part of this process of becoming a work of art. As I mentioned in a prior passage, this book will give you the tools to carve a masterpiece like no other. However, you first need to see yourself through the vantage point of importance and as a commodity like silver, gold or precious stones. Regardless of the number of students on your campus however plentiful or few, your presence brings with it a specific level of expectation. Your presence adds to the lifeblood of your institution. If no one returned to your school, your institution would face a possibility of shutting down because it would not be fiscally feasible to sustain itself. Your tuition dollars are a precious resource (commodity) in short supply and high demand. You should have more to show for it than merely a receipt. Expect more than just being a consumer of learning. Consider this.

When you go into a store or business for a product or service, you expect a few things:

- An atmosphere of assistance in getting the product or service desired
- The provider knowing you enough to make the connection with what you need

- Questions about the product or service will be answered by their trained staff so you clearly understand what you are getting for your money
- An ability to check in or check back with the provider to assist with any troubleshooting when a situation comes up that you need some level of follow-up
- A product or service that will provide you the results you are looking for you to achieve the need or desire
- A willingness to pay for the product or service you are receiving

As an example, if I eat at a restaurant and I order steak and it is overcooked, do I settle for the way it was prepared, or do I get it the way I ordered my ribeye? Of course, I am going to ask my server for another ribeye the way that I like it. If I go and buy a computer, I am going to get the laptop that is best for me. If I run into a problem, I ask for help to better understand how the computer works so that I can use it the way I want. The same is true if I am getting a pair of pants altered at a tailor. The alterations are going to be specific to the way I want the pants to fit in the waist, inseam, and length.

Is there a difference between what I have offered about ordering a steak, buying a computer, or tailoring a pair of slacks and going to college? The answer is NO. The process is a little different, but the result is still the same. Let me explain:

- Education is a product or service that you want or need
- The university admissions process makes sure you are the right fit and offers programs and services that attract you to them, highlighting preparation and outcomes

- Based on their decision(s) you select a college that meets your needs (price, major, location, school pride, legacy, atmosphere, etc.)
- The university charges you for all the products or services you use to obtain the degree
- The university invests in aesthetics, intellectual resources, and hires specialized service providers to fulfill these roles
- You then seek out those specific resources in order to get what you need (professor office hours, career services, writing labs, tutors, guidance and advice from academic advisors, etc.)
- If all goes as planned, and you meet their academic standards returning year after year (retention) as a loyal customer, a degree is attained

The moment you accept their offer and attend the institution, YOU are their client.

Promises, Promises

Are you getting the level of service you need? Tactfully, demand more, settle for nothing less, and utilize all the services available at your institution. If for no other reason than for the gain that it will provide you over the span of your life and access to all that you aspire to be. When you really think about it, would you spend over $100,000.00 and not have anything to show for it? It means that with every fiber of your body, you are to expect that the university will live up to its promises. Among those service promise makers are the President, Provost, Student Affairs, Professors, and the list goes on.

Anything short of your needs being met is insufficient and as the client you are to let them know. The conversation is staged by you identifying the void or question and working in partnership with them to address the concern. This is a process that gets repeated from matriculation to graduation. This process is called retention (a returning loyal customer). It is no different than going to your favorite restaurant and patronizing them because of the connection they have successfully created for you as a customer when ordering a steak just the way you like it.

Remember, your institution must maintain your standards as the client. If a college or university does not live up to its deliverables, options include transferring to a better service provider. Take advantage of all there is to offer and upon your completion they will call you an excellent "loyal client," an alumna! As a student, you are the lifeblood of the institution. On a campus where thousands of students enter year after year, no institution can afford to lose you because they were unable to fulfill their part of this partnership. You have a voice, so do not lose sight of this important concept. Get what you came to get specifically tailored to you.

Your New Gig

College, believe it or not, is a full-time job. Not in the way you may think of it as work at the pool, grocery store, office or any summer hustle you have worked over the summer to put some spending money in your pocket. This may be the only occupation that you work full time and pay someone to be there. You do not get paid to go to school (unless you have a scholarship). There is no clock to punch into, and you don't have to log your billable hours. However, it is important that you have something to show for your effort - graduation!

You are coming to your institution of higher learning to do just that, learn. Your primary job is to arrive, find something you are passionate about, and meet the basic requirements illustrating your knowledge of a specific skill/talent from school making yourself marketable to a future employer. This means your approach to it should be to mirror the type of career you want to become "the best" at i.e. teacher, accountant, social worker, etc." You will read, write, test, study and do this for nine months out of a year for the next four years. So how does a college student with a full-time employee mentality approach this new venture?

Here are several things I brainstormed:

- Be committed to the process of getting trained and open to new ideas.
- Your supervisors (professors, advisors, deans, administrators, etc.) know more than you and you should listen to wisdom and advice from them.
- Showing up to work is the only option. There are no days off or missed classes.
- Be a team player. You live among people from all over the world.
- Always do your best and seek excellence.
- Don't just meet expectations, look to exceed them. This is how influential people will find you. This is how you get noticed for your work.
- Be on time for meetings (classes). This disruptive behavior will get you noticed for all the wrong reasons.
- Always be prepared. So, if called upon to offer your commentary, a question or otherwise, participate in the process.

- Sacrifices and diligence are always necessary. Make sure the choice matches the outcome you want to live with.
- Spending extra time on your job is essential to your success, and you may have to realign your priorities as needed.
- This job comes with lots of evaluations and assessments. Will you be ready?
- Given your track record, would you hire yourself? Is a layoff, PIP (Performance Improvement Plan), or being fired in your future based on your performance?

Your approach to going to college has so many benefits to it that if you position yourself for greatness, it will find you. This may not be your only obligation, yet, it is one of the most important to pay careful attention to completing; so, do not squander the opportunity for anyone or anything. Remember all those individuals who have poured into you, like Nina mentioned earlier.

Return on Your Investment

The investment you are about to make is immense now. It is costly whether you have a trust, scholarship, college fund, or are piecing it together. Be glad you have the opportunity. Many young people, due to things they are unable to control, have the intellect to pursue their dreams and not always the financial resources. Some have the resources and are unable to dedicate themselves to the experience due to a myriad of other roadblocks. It will challenge you in ways you cannot imagine beyond money. You will have to use critical thinking, set priorities, sacrifice, and at times pure grit to get things done. The quest is for you to now have a return on your investment. Someone has instilled the raw materials in you and now this next phase is completely up to you. Will you put in the work? As you look across the landscape, tuitions are continuing to rise and for the average student the cost for college is now no less than $100K. That is quite a grip. It is also an investment of your time, ability to stay focused on your goal, and many sacrifices that will insure the full maturation of the investment. As a degree holder, you stand to make multiple times the amount of money over your lifetime than an individual without a college degree. The amount of opportunities available to you to change or augment your career aspirations will not stop. It will just be a matter of gaining new exposure to information and technology to enhance your credentials.

Access to More

This degree or advanced degrees will open so many doors for you in that way. Jonathan, who received a degree in Sociology, is now working in the nonprofit sector as a project manager seeking to grant younger students' access to educational opportunities. Corrine whose interest is in gerontology (study and scientific knowledge of caring for older age individuals) now has her own business and is working as a consultant with families partnering their older members of their family with the proper facility or level of care. Shawn, an Education major, trains and evaluates new teachers entering the field of education as they secure their teaching credential. Karl, a Business major, works as a team manager and relationship specialist facilitating partnerships with colleges and universities creating online graduate programs. Dana, an International Relations major with a love and passion for sports as a former college athlete, has gone from working with The United States Olympic Basketball Team to now working as a Basketball Operations Manager for a WNBA team. Cassandra a liberal arts major became a trained teacher and with her advanced degrees in curriculum development is now an owner of her own company working with school administrators training faculty and professionals at colleges and charter schools on cutting edge pedagogy. Jessica, a Nutrition major, has finessed all that she has learned into becoming a Human Resources guru and is consulting on the side as individuals seek her knowledge and insight on best hiring practices for their organizations. These are former students and current professionals that I know who have reaped the fruits of their labor by making deliberate decisions years ago that continued the cycle of opportunity and success. I want you to be a part of this inclusive club. Borrowing a principle from the Bible, you do reap (produce) what you sow (plant). If you do not plant, it will not grow.

This tipping point is where Nina and I started from in our coaching session. Among other things explained, getting into college does present itself as a challenge. I do not deny this. Some schools admit only 10 percent of their incoming applicants. This presents its own set of issues for students. Yet, once you are in, you can face even greater odds of success. The rate of success continues to be unsettling. Completion rates are nearing 50%. Retention and attainment rates continue to shrink for all students and are at disparaging rates across many socioeconomic and demographic categories. The reasons, while countless, include preparation, cost, degree selection, and the list go on and on; I believe it has more to do with what students do when they get to their institution of higher learning. Take Denise for example. She is a well-prepared student from a stable middle-class environment and a decent school. Being a Pre-Med major, she took on a heavy load her first semester in order to keep on track with going to Med School at a prestigious university. Her first term includes Biology, Chemistry, Physics, English, and Calculus with two labs. Ultimately, all the statistical data in the world does not make anyone feel any better when they must seek other alternatives to what they started.

The journey of college success is about preparation. Yet, the fact remains to your institution of choice that they made a calculated risk regarding your candidacy given the prior record you produced – test scores, academic courses, extracurricular activities, etc. Although stressful and cumbersome, this process took approximately a calendar year to finalize. You are here now, so how do you get through the next four or five years successfully? I am convinced it is based on the habits you discover and establish hour by hour, day by day, and week by week until you graduate. For as easy as it seems, many well prepared students have arrived, struggled and gone back home, or needed to transfer. Christopher, for example, put himself in an excellent position coming from his successful high school career. His arrival at the university was now a chance to experience his newfound freedom and continue his previous success; instead he became a social butterfly on campus. He joined only a few organizations, and they became his priority verses working to reestablish the good habits he used to get him into school. A missed class here and there, oversleeping for a midterm, and a lackluster term paper meant he went from a highflyer to academic probation and losing scholarships that he earned. His lack of focus and priority setting was his downfall that he now must overcome.

Yet, many students less prepared can soar, and make a long-lasting impact maneuvering to the next level of growth and accomplishment. No, I do not think it is luck. There is a certain something that is incorporated into their being which has made all the difference. Lorriece, who came to the Summer Program that I directed was not as savvy as her cohort members, but she was a student ready to go and hit the ground running. She knew what she lacked and worked to fill the void. She was in the face of her professors and me. She utilized the countless campus resources that I identified would help increase her skills. She knew that if she did not complete the summer program successfully, she was at risk of not being able to return in the fall. We met weekly to hear of her trials and triumphs as she pursued her degree. Despite her lack of preparation, it did not prevent her from the proactive approach she took to get the job done, establish herself, and replicate this over and over. Likewise, I was not the best student. My SATs were just average. I had mostly college prep courses, was ranked in the top third of my class, and really did not push myself to my fullest potential. I did just enough to get by with average grades and now possess a master's degree. Nothing aligned me for guaranteed success given my track record. I made many mistakes and did some pretty immature things that did not allow me to recover, sometimes falling flat. Yet here I am about to drop you some knowledge. Go figure!

Praise in Public

Before I go any further, it is important to offer this specific message for your parents and supporters. Going to college is a privilege, but by no means a right. It is true given the world we are in now that college is a necessity to get ahead in life. You need to cherish this opportunity and make the most of it. Many people have made countless and unknown sacrifices to put you in the position you are in now. As my father has said to me countless times and still holds true today, "In life you sometimes only get one bite of the apple." Simply put, make the most of every opportunity because they do not always come in multiples. This really resonated for me as I began to work with students. I have been in countless conversations with families at admissions visits, university receptions, open houses, parent's weekends, and other opportunities and heard the backstory from parents talking to me about the kind of sacrifices being made to put their children through school.

They are working multiple jobs, taking extra shifts, borrowing insane amounts of money, taking out second mortgages, and at times doing without to make this all possible for their precious commodity, you. Tears were beginning to well in the eyes of one single parent mother as she described the opportunity for her son. She said, "I have worked my fingers to the bone and have made this possible for Shawn. I need my baby to do his work and have a degree in his hands so that he does not have to work as hard as I have had to all my life. I am going to struggle some back at home, but I do not want him to worry here, and just get his studies done." Opportunities missed can alter the trajectory of many lives. The greatest gift you can give yourself and your family is to return each semester more determined than you were the last. This makes the sacrifice worth it in more ways than you will ever know. When your parents go to work and church or other places and someone asks, "How is Shawn doing?" There is no greater sense of pride for your parent to be able to say, "Yes, Shawn is doing well. He is in his second semester and doing great. He made the Dean's List." It is a proud moment for them every time. Pause and please take a moment now to thank your parent(s) for this opportunity.

The Old College Try

Regardless of whether you have the pedigree or not, your use of this advice won't guarantee success. Nothing does. However, whenever you apply it, it will create an opportunity to see things in a new prism. Kelvin, who is one of the fondest students that I have worked with over my time, was a first-generation student from a single parent family. He struggled horribly his first semesters when we began working together. He seemed to fight me and ultimately himself tooth and nail about everything. He knew some but clearly not enough. His grades were just average, but he could do great things. One Friday night his first weekend or two on campus after a social I helped chaperon, I thought he was ready to throw in the towel and crumble under the pressure of it all. So, I hired him as a student worker in my office. Instead of telling him, I offered live examples from myself and others I knew who would take him under their wing. Once he lightened his load and worked through some baggage holding him back, he became an instant leader both inside and outside of the classroom. He did not back down from the challenges and the rest is another living legacy of recreating himself despite the odds. He is now a lawyer and family man. I do not claim to know it all, but as I did for Kelvin, I offer a lot from first-hand experience and pass it on to the thousands of students that I have had the privilege to work with over my career span. If you can learn from my mistakes or missteps I have seen many make and at least recognize them, the light bulb will illuminate at the right time giving you a chance to approach the crossroad and choose a fork in the road that makes the most sense. The decision will be what is best and right for you. I would offer your success has as much to do with your ability to apply these simple principles that increase your work ethic and the level of connection you have to your institution (classmates, advisors, faculty, mentors, etc.) than anything else.

If you are ready to make it happen, so am I, let's get started.

Chapter 4

Lesson 2:
College, is NOT High School

There is so much to take in and stimuli abound in your first hours of arriving at college. There will be much glam and glitter with your institution providing a welcome that compares to no other. In great anticipation of your arrival, ambassadors, students, organizations, and administrators offer the red carpet to your new home in hopes that you soon claim your school as your own. This is not done as an illusion or smoke and mirrors. The intent is to help you during the biggest transition you will make by providing many of the basics in the beginning to establish yourself. Where is your residence hall? Who is your roommate? What is the name of your Resident Assistant (RA) and Hall Director? Where is the closest or best dining hall located? Finally, you make one last run to the local store in the area to get groceries and supplies to make the finishing touches to your room. Informal and formal ceremonies mark the moment that you have officially matriculated into your institution.

The Home Stretch

As the new beginning creeps in, an unseen chapter is about to close. Your final goodbyes to family are front and center. Whether you are anxiously looking to whisk your parents away or dreading your final good-byes, outright freedom and independence is on the other side of the ledger. It is time to patiently hear all of the armchair advice you may have heard again on the car ride to campus or the many side conversations during other parts of summer; (try not to roll your eyes, or mouth the words your parents say word for word behind their backs, or offer too many deep sighs.) During matriculation ceremonies as the President of the College or Provost offers words of welcome prior to the dismissal of parents from campus, I have seen many a final lecture from moms and dads. "We love you and want you to do well. Please call us often and let us know how you are doing." "Study hard and make us proud." "Manage your time and responsibilities and bring home some decent grades." "Focus, focus." Long embraces and sobs between tears by students or parents have blanketed many campuses annually. I ran into The Lewis' as they made their walk to the empty SUV, thanking me for my support. A handshake or hug, my business card, a calming stare into their eyes accompany these words of assurance to them every time, "I will be watching out for your baby!" I clearly saw that despite the age or maturity of their student, they clearly belong to someone and letting go never comes easy. This reality was even more poignant for me when I became a parent and watched my own children head off to college. It is hard to let go. Regardless of how you feel about the message or the messenger, there are good things to take away from the discussions. Accept the fact that your parent(s) or guardians understand the impact of all you have been given, the ethics they have instilled, and what this unknown journey will look like for you - a blank slate awaiting your touch. This is their first time in your life that they are truly sitting on the sidelines watching you. Their input is still accessible, but not in the same manner. You are now in charge of you! You are now on your own and going to be ultimately held accountable for every decision you make. It is not a bad thing. It is just the reality of being where you are at this point in your life - in college. There will be ways you are prepared, and ways you think you are prepared, and at times you are not prepared and just do not know it yet.

Now It Is Real

As a Resident Assistant in the residence halls on my floor, we were trained and mindful to be aware of the signs of a student being homesick and feeling the blues as the transition for them became more apparent. I would see students like Freshman Gabe or Kevin from small Indiana towns either in a closed-door room or just alone at mealtimes. Regardless of where you come from everyone can get homesick. The idea was to connect them with other students without shaming them aloud that they were feeling disengaged from their new home. I am convinced that this part of the transition to college is the most pivotal for you. It has nothing to do with your previous data points, awards, or accolades. Now that you are on your own, what is important for you in establishing yourself? What do you need to do to be prepared to fully immerse yourself academically and every other facet of your new life to be successful?

Do you understand the differences between high school and college? In many respects the two are as different as apples to oranges:

- In high school, you are on a specific schedule set by others. In college, you set your own.
- In high school, you may have had a curfew, and in college you don't.
- In high school, someone will check up on you to make sure you complete your work and make sure you turn it in. In college, it is no big deal to them if you do or don't, either is okay.
- In high school, you take all subjects. In college, you take what you like and fulfill requirements for what you want to be.
- In high school if you skip class, a school official or parent is notified. In college, attendance is likely not taken; however, you are still responsible for the information.
- High school is a requirement and is covered financially, and college is a choice that you make. You pay for every course, book, and student fees/activities.
- In high school, you complete all your homework in one night, and in college you always have homework that takes more than one night to finish.
- High school work gets dictated by someone else. College work is assigned or offered on your syllabus. It is up to you to keep track of your homework.
- In high school, no one manages your time. In college you manage your time, you work and your play; just make sure you work more than you play. Work life balance is an important concept.
- In high school, you get progress reports at midterms, and in college there are no progress reports.
- In high school, there are typically several tests spread throughout the semester, and in college you can have a midterm and final only.

- In high school your behaviors and actions like fighting or other violations can get you suspended or expelled with an opportunity to recover from your mistake and still have some options to get your education. In college certain violations like plagiarism, use of alcohol or other disturbances can lead to immediate suspension, dismissal and additional consequences impacting your future access to education.
- In high school, low academic performance can prevent you from participating in sports or activities. In college, poor performance can result in academic probation, suspension, dismissal, and ineligibility from financial aid.

To Do List(s)

Are these the thoughts that may be milling through your mind as your parents drive off farther and farther away? The reality is still the same - you are here now, so what's next? Again, either way, your start date is a ticking clock closer to some of the following things you need to have in place. There is no specific order, and this is not a complete list, but there is a lot to do in making sure you have a great start:

1. Buying course materials
2. Finding your classrooms
3. Getting your class schedule
4. Figuring out the dining schedule
5. Understanding the residence hall rules
6. Figuring out and utilizing the campus resources available
7. Reading through syllabi
8. Seeing Advisor

9. Locating key resources
10. Attending mandatory workshops/orientation sessions
11. Securing funds from Financial Aid
12. Working with the Student Accounts
13. Roommate chat about room rules (yes, have this conversation)
14. Completing homework (if assigned) especially over the summer
15. Establishing a schedule
16. Having fun
17. Meeting new people
18. The list goes on and on......

Scavenger Hunt

It's important when you start to keep perspective when you're transitioning to your new environment. Remember, you don't have to have all the answers. Your quest is to find the resources and respond accordingly. Believe it or not, it will take at least six to eight weeks to get accustomed to your new environment. With all the understanding of your schedule and organizing you will need to do, be comfortable with being uncomfortable and realize that you do not have to have it all together. The key to this process is to do so in increments. Break it down from a boulder to pebbles. A boulder is too heavy to carry around day to day. However, it is easier to put in the work to break down the boulder into pieces that are easier to transport such as creating your own schedule for classes, establishing homework habits, meeting new friends, and connecting with all the activities your campus offers. In other words, manage and squash the feelings of being homesick; find your comfort in all the habits and rituals that you have acquired at your school and home. As easy as it is to do, don't go home for the weekends early on. There is so much you miss out on and you end up on a continual cycle of catching up to those who are better adjusted than you are. The isolation creates more distance between your classmates and adds a multiplier effect to your adjustment process. Typically, the isolation begins to leak into other parts of your life, including your academic performance. These situations do not happen independent of each other. Your institution thinks this is a good idea. Your Parents Weekend is typically at least 6 to 8 weeks from the start of school. Unless it is imperative, try to persist on campus. It will make all the difference. Felicia, a freshman, was dating a high school senior in her hometown. She made the trip back and forth weekend after weekend. The distance became too much, and they parted ways. As she reset herself to her campus environment, it was difficult to join in the social interaction because her peers did not know her well enough to connect and include her in their activities. While I understand your loyalty to your companion, it is important to establish yourself in the new environment where most of your time will be spent. Social connections are imperative to establish and maintain. Felicia saw the void and made the proper adjustment, but it was more difficult because she was not immediately engaged in her new environment.

Bloom and Ripples

Establishing a network of support is an important step in adjusting. Step back for a moment and think. You were among the top people and connected so well in your high school. You knew most if not all the teachers in your school and several members of the senior class or underclassmen.

People in your school looked to you as an influencer offering insight and perspective you learned in your time there in class, organizations, sports, and other activities. This may not have been your immediate impact as a freshman, but you evolved into the roles you were in. It did not happen overnight (maybe it did). Regardless, you took the opportunity to advance and offer a cumulative picture of yourself. Believe it or not, this is the same process you need to go through now at college. You are starting at square one. Continuing with the rock metaphor, do you want to have the impact of a pebble being thrown in an ocean or a boulder tossed in a pond? Both will make ripples in the water, but one is just more visible to the naked eye. You ultimately can choose. This is again the precursor to the rest of your life. There are hundreds of free resources on campus that go untapped. These free services help you carve your work of art. You are the stone block and each resource helps you chip away and offer fine details to create a rendering like no other. From Career Services as early as your freshman year to writing, math, and science labs or tutoring. The most important thing to keep in mind is not having the answers. Those will come with time. It is, however, knowing where and whom to connect with to get them. For example, the Office of Multicultural Student Services typically has resources which help you tie your connection to the university based on your cultural identity. Cultural and social programming, the ability to hold officer roles within the organization, academic and support counseling, and working in their office as an assistant, are among many ways this office creates connections for you to take advantage of as a student. All these opportunities I tried to create for my students in a previous role as director. Try something new or try to develop prior skills that benefit others. With a sound foundation, you can create your own identity by giving yourself permission to blossom with all the potential you can muster. As you create the new and improved you, wipe the slate clean and stop playing the same recording in your mind of what you cannot do and in your new environment, "Give it the good old <u>college try.</u>" Remember, you are developing all the character traits and skills for people to be able to recognize you out of a crowd from this point on. Do not cater your skills to fit the audience but stay true to who you are, and people will be drawn to you based on your character. So, in order to make an impact on your college experience (boulder), break it down to smaller productive parts (pebble). Find organizations, clubs or activities which will allow you to exhibit your talents. If it does not exist on campus, here is your chance to produce it. Individuals will gravitate to things they are passionate about like your new organization. By doing so, you create a space where you can make an impact (boulder) on your college environment (pond). The greater the splash, the greater the impact on your campus. Do you want to be one among the many students on campus or known for the skills and talents you possess? Cherish every opportunity possible to stand out. Yes, be outstanding! Make some splashes and ripples. As you embark on this journey that will have many twists and turns, trials and triumphs, tests and testimonies, know that you have the resources available to you. It is your job to connect to the university and see this relationship as a partnership instead of just being a college student. You are honestly so much more than this and should expect more out of yourself.

Chapter 5

Lesson 3:
Establishing Your Foundation

Goal-Setting

It is important to know what you are focused on in order to know if you accomplished what you set out to do. What is important to you? Not to your parents, mentors, or anyone else. What is important to you? Remember, this is your experience, and not anyone else's. You get to create and direct this experience for yourself. Goal setting can:

- Provide vision
- Direct your path (next steps)
- Instill motivation
- Stretch you beyond your comfort zone to new levels of achievement

Without goals you stand a chance of:

- Low grades
- Performing below your potential
- No accountability partners
- Frustration
- Quitting

Goals can specify and define your direction. They chart a course of action much like picking a destination on a map. Are you taking the best or fastest route to get there? Goal setting offers continuous feedback on your progress and allows you to adjust moving forward - not excuses which tend to stagnate your momentum. You must control your own destiny and not be sidetracked by allowing someone or something to take you off course. Once you have achieved the goal, it is necessary to have others. If you seek to get a 3.0 GPA your first term and it happens, what do you do the other seven semesters? Clearly you are not done. You would minimally seek another 3.0 and likely shoot for something higher the next semester. Now consider expanding your social network by joining organizations or developing mentoring relationships with faculty in your department. Approached properly, you will have lots to do between now and graduation.

Author YOUR story

As you set your goals for yourself, here is one approach:

1. Set a goal - choose something that YOU want to achieve. Write it down somewhere you will see it daily.
2. Write a plan of action. The "act" is figuring out how you are going to achieve the larger goal. Successfully completing these small steps is progress towards the stated goal. It should have dates attached to it.
3. Follow your plan (actions) toward your goal. Be able to ask yourself are you meeting your mini acts and meeting deadlines? If not, adjust so that you get there.
4. Once achieved, set another goal. Follow the previous process and success will become a habit that you develop continuously.

Chapter 6

Lesson 4:
Time Management: The Make or Break

So, let's break this down now. You have 168 hours per week (7 days x 24 hours). Whether you use time well or not, it is going to keep moving on with or without you. The choices you make and do not make (this is an action also) are decisions that carry rewards or consequences attached to them. Thinking of your decisions about how you use your time as only a yes or a no is not enough. This impacts every aspect of your life as a college student. It affects your schedule, the pacing you need to complete other homework, and the potential sacrifices you have made to catch up. The mental anguish is more than you expect causing undue stress. No one works well under pressure. If you start working on an assignment late, it means either substandard work or a rushed job. You know it when you present it, and trust me, so does your professor grading your assignments. By no means does it mean that you must study all the time. This opposite extreme is not the answer. What you may gain in knowledge, you miss out on forming connections. All the wisdom in the world makes no difference if you cannot communicate it or network with individuals who can help you develop or share what you know. Understanding the importance of time management means you will not waste countless hours on frivolous things.

Blinders Necessary

There are always distractions which prevent you from focusing. When I have worked with students, this has many times been the focus of our conversation. One of my former students, Renee, came to me because she was on academic probation. My role was to sit on an academic standards board for the college, then work with the students identified and help them achieve above a 2.0 or greater to continue in school. In our one-on-one meeting, she offered so many reasons why she was not studying. "I was talking with my roommates and not studying until it was too late. I just started dating Jalen." "I was not doing well in the class, so I just stop going!" "I overslept because I stayed up all night the night before." "The big game and dance were this weekend." I could not tell you all the excuses why she and other students did not manage their time better and make better decisions. Students who are less productive and less organized do not use their time wisely. Once you understand how time impacts your day to day operations as a student, you will redirect your priorities to make sure it either fits within your schedule or can wait. When you eliminate the time wasters (it can wait) your time becomes much more productive and you accomplish more in each timeframe or assigned task. Regardless of the ability or the smarts a student possesses, once we broke this down so Renee could see the impact, it informed her intentions with using time properly. Time management effectively used will make a good student stronger and will give a student not doing so well the ability to make positive strides to improve.

Distracted

My time management started from a bad place and evolved considerably from hard knocks to eventually a string of victories. Let me explain as we break it down to how you can apply it in your own life. I was a student who did not really work hard in high school, and despite my lack of effort found myself in the top third of my class. I took the minimum college prep curriculum and scored an average SAT score to attend the one college that I applied. I had grandiose ideas of my next steps in life and no idea how hard I would need to work to make it happen. I thought I wanted to go to college to be a lawyer. I majored in Political Science and minored in Criminal Justice. This seemed straight forward enough. I signed up for classes and took 14 credit hours. I had College Algebra, English Composition, a Family Housing course and Geography course. These courses filled requirements and were things that I was interested in given the kinds of courses left for a first-year student. This was by no means a tough or heavy load. I lived in a major hub of activity. My residence hall was part of a complex that had at least 10 coed dorms, a large dining hall, a snack bar, and an arcade that everyone frequented. There were thousands of people for a social butterfly like myself to meet, and I did. I was smart enough to attend all my classes, but as soon as class was over, I was in the mix of hanging out, intramurals, playing ball, talking to everyone and making many social connections. I did the minimum in the way of homework and very little studying until I had to do so (which meant it was too late or I was not as prepared as I could have been.) I was never ahead and at best just on schedule. As an early riser for morning classes, I was awake by 7 am and in bed as late as 1am in the morning. Usually hanging out for a minimum of two or three hours per night from 10 pm on until I could not take it anymore. Again, the concept of studying or developing my academic work ethic hit me on occasion when midterms or a final draft of papers were due. My level of preparation on a scale from 1 to 10 was no better than a 6. I had glimpses of looking the part with high visibility in the study lounge at the top of the hallway, but by no means living it to my limits. I attended dance parties offered by the Black fraternities and sororities, but never attended any off-campus parties and did not drink at all – yes, it is possible. By the time I finished the first term I had 3 Cs and a B. A cumulative 2.142 GPA. I was not in any academic danger because a 2.0 is the minimum needed to be out of academic peril. However, I was not breaking any records and far from the Dean's List.

Easy Way Out

So, as you can see from the description, I had no direction, drive or vision for where I needed to be. Time was just a commodity that was always going to be there. There were multiple competing priorities that were at play and the path of least resistance was always the easiest choice to make. The fact that I found others to hang and waste time with gave my bandwagon mentality life. Everyone was doing what I was doing, and I was doing what others were doing. Looking studious in the study lounge was more about status and not standard. It was giving me the appearance of mastering my work while all it really was is an exercise in mediocrity that I used to convince myself that I studied so hard and spent a lot of time doing it. Many times, during a marathon session, I was asleep in my book, daydreaming, and unable to remember what I read or looking at a completely highlighted yellow page of every word being an important component to explain a specific concept or theory. But if you asked me about the latest gossip or other trivial useless bits of info on the latest break-up between two people, the latest dance moves, great party or an album release, I could tell you. I was up on all the latest social happenings in everyone else's life and not present for the most important thing: an education and preparation for my life aspirations.

Epiphany

I was capable of more and I was shortchanging myself. I was my own problem between falling asleep in my book, taking forever to read a chapter from losing my place, and being distracted by people walking by the study lounge window of the door waving at me. Up to this point, I did not have to work hard or be strategic in how I did things; I just did what was necessary to minimally satisfy the requirement. Oh yeah, I forgot that I was having so much fun at college and studying minimally! If my effort was an average or a good grade, it mattered some but not enough to make me change my ways or take a good and hard look in the mirror. Self-reflection was never my thing. My natural intelligence was only the start of the process and on its own did not make me smarter. It is how you apply it that really made the difference, and I was finally making the connection to the problem and the secret to my eventual success. I was good and did not really know how to get better. During one particular study session, I saw someone in my study lounge getting things done in the same amount of time it took me to get started. It finally dawned on me that I was not as organized and only offered minimal effort. I was not tracking the work from classes and keeping it in a place where I could go to it readily. My peers in my circle were not smarter than me, they just applied themselves better and exhibited more discipline than me. I was just half-stepping through college. Between terms, I found a few things I needed. I found a free university issued spiral bound calendar, and a "Things I Gotta Do List." I tried this in my second and third terms. This was the start of my seeking to reach my full potential by being more organized. During these terms, I began to improve my study habits and make some actual effort to do more than homework – yes, study and be prepared. I stepped up my game and realized that I was not better in school because I was not smart; I had a good memory, was a good listener, and at times could use the two to remember parts of lectures or words on a chalkboard to recall info on tests or quizzes. I put in extra time beyond completing assignments. I studied in microbursts studying for specific intervals (idle times between classes, and early on weekends, after dinner until time for bed 7 pm - 12 midnight) and took short breaks until I understood what I needed to know. Studying with partners on occasion, I could breakdown info into pieces that made sense to other students and my explanations stuck with me. I made sacrifices to not go out with friends or hang out like I had previously. Trust me, I wanted to go. I was finally able to hear the voice inside clearly now saying, "You have to do what you know is best for # 1, me." "Stop taking the easy way out and doing like everyone else." "With these new habits I am able to see the fruits of my labor now. "Doing this a few times and seeing the benefits reinforced my decisions. Finally, the GPA began to rise to just about a 2.5 and I began to see more Bs than Cs. The third term, I did put in more time studying after I fractured a bone in my foot playing basketball. I really took a step back and reflected on the amount of time I wasted, and I studied even more. Still not at my full capacity yet, I knew the secret I had kept from myself and my success was TIME and EFFORT.

Priority with Purpose

Balance and perspective became the equalizer. By this I mean I had no prioritizing ability and I had the ability to say "yes" to everything. "No" is an okay word also, and it took me some time to understand its full meaning. Here is an example. I may have a paper due on Monday that was assigned the previous week. In the days in between, I worked on a draft, but it is rough and needs to be developed. Peer reviews may help some, but unfortunately, they are not equipped to help like my professor. My professor's office hours are right after my last class of the day two days out of the week. Their office is a few minutes' walk across campus. Instead of going to see them, I opt to take a nap for a couple of hours each day after class because of my late nights with friends or going to parties and watching football Saturday and Sunday. The two hour naps may have helped me rest from all of the wasted time from the previous days; however, the amount of time to get the draft looked at and receive some necessary feedback is only 20 minutes and will offer better insight on my next steps to write the best paper possible. What was most important in this moment? Of course, your paper is the priority. However, look at the missed opportunities that happened twice. A walk to their office after classes ended for assistance. A professor will never tell you exactly what to write; that is not their role in this context. The commentary they offer will be more broad strokes of what I should do to capture the prose offered. Now I am functioning at half capacity and going to expend a lot of time and energy at the detriment of writing the paper and the coursework from my other classes I put on hold to complete this assignment. When you do not manage your time properly, it has a cause and effect impact on everything immediate, long term, and beyond. None of these things independent of each other is a problem. It is, however, the cumulative impact which can influence the outcome of not saying "no." Manage your time so time does not manage you.

An organization I worked with in Indianapolis while at Butler University called the Center for Leadership Development-a non-profit organization that preps high school students for excellence and higher education. Ms. Helen Baker had a time proverb that I learned. In honor of CLD, I have every group I have spoken to or taught recite this because it is so powerful and a good mantra to live by in relation to managing time properly. It is the following:

In Time,

On Time,

Every Time,

Except when ahead of Time,

That's better Time

Tips

Managing your time means having work and play balance. Both work and play should be deliberate but not operate in extremes. Start by doing the following:

1. Do what need to be done so you can do what you want. In other words, set proper priorities. It may mean that the need (reading two chapters due tomorrow) and your want (going to the free movie for two hours) don't match. Managing your time so you can complete the necessary tasks is always first, and then have the fun.
2. Create a daily to do list. There is no sense working hard and not knowing all that needs to be done. The one

thing you can depend on as a constant is homework and studying. Don't lose track of it. When you finish an assignment, check it off, and put a line through it. It is a great feeling to complete it.

3. Set start and finish times. My study time as often as I could was 7 pm - midnight. I took breaks as needed and really tried to hold to this schedule. At 12am, I stopped and before I went to bed, I made the to-do list based on what I had not finished that evening and the next assignments.

4. Pace your time. If you have an assignment that is going to take longer, work on it in smaller bursts of time. Working on it daily is a good practice. No need to cram or rush. Your best work is done when you set the right conditions. With proper planning, you can break an assignment that is offered a week earlier into segments over several days. No one works well under pressure. At some point it catches up with you.

5. Chunking is an important concept to keep in mind concerning your time. Working daily is important, and what you accomplish in each setting is part of the process. What can you complete in one hour? Draft of an outline for a paper, read a chapter, rewrite your notes, or make flashcards for a test you are preparing for soon. There is no sense in taking the time to study if what you're doing is squandering the time daydreaming or being distracted by your phone vibrating at you to respond to a less important text or post!

6. Seek help when necessary. Although not directly related to time, this means being resourceful so that you use your time wisely and get the guidance or direction from the professor, teaching assistant, or tutorial center. There is no worse feeling than getting

ready to work and not being able to figure it out or not knowing where to start. It all equates to wasted time. Be honest with yourself and time. Make sure you know how to so you can do it.

7. Set a duration for an effective use of time. This is like developing a muscle. Start with say 20-30 minutes of studying and then take a short break. Return and repeat the same time interval. As you adjust, you will add more time and thus be focused and increase your stamina. You will want to get to the point when you can work for 60 minutes nonstop or more.

8. Idle time can be productive time. Create flashcards, go see a tutor, or read a portion of a chapter during times you are not in class or working. It may be minutes or hours but make it productive to use your time as greatly as you can. Remember time is the one thing you always use or lose and never get back.

9. Make adjustments when necessary. Life happens and you may not always keep the pattern. If you switch it up, you know you must make up the time somewhere.

10. Figure out the amount of "white space" in your life. Set up your schedule and write it on a paper grid. Include meals, class times, work, commuting, hygiene, sleep, etc. Once all your obligations are accounted for, the white space in your grid is open time to study. Remember all of it does not need to be planned, but you should have as much planned as it takes given your demands and availability.

11. Your study time should be twice the amount of credit hours you are taking per semester. 15 credit hours means 30 hours of study over the span of the week – minimum. 30 hours spread out over 7 days is 4+ hours per day. Over 6 days (which is what I recommend, and

a day of rest) is 5 hours per day. 30 hours studying is less than 20% of your total time in the week 168 hours.

12. Do not procrastinate. Putting off your homework/studying only piles it onto other assignments and interferes with the progress you can make day to day. Start it now, not later.

13. Finally, the greatest time consumer of the modern era. **Put down your phone.** Yes, please put it away in another room far from your workspace and not only on silent or vibrate. This may be the difference between productivity and your demise. It can wait. Use it as a study break or wait until you are done with what you are working on. TTYL! Let your inner circle know that during your designated study time, they can only contact you if it is an emergency. People will respect your commitment.

Find the Time

One of my students I taught as an instructor at Northern Virginia Community College named Liz had a conversation with me after class. She was struggling now because of her time management. Liz is holding down a job and taking four classes. "I am not sure how to manage my time or get some of it back?" In our chat, there was very little margin for her to work with to recoup some of her time and complete homework better. I then asked her about her screen time. "Liz, how much time do you spend on your phone?" "My phone?", she looked puzzled. "Yes, your phone. Go to your settings and tell me how much screen time you average?" Liz went to her phone settings and with a bit of an amazed look, offered "I spend about 7 hours." I asked, "How much time do you spend studying based on your time management assignment from the previous week? Now, take your screen time, cut it in half, and add three- and one-half hours to your study time. While it may take time to adjust your habits, it will make you more productive", I offered.

I coach students now who have so many more distractions to deal with, and it is impossible to not use a phone in the modern era. It can be limited so that it does not occupy so much of your time. Shawn, a former client and I, had this discussion about the phone and being so attached to it. We used a work/reward process. Study and accomplish an assignment and check your phone once it is complete. She was able to focus and finish homework with much more favorable results including weaning herself from her phone.

Some of these concepts will be incorporated when study skills and tips come up later.

Chapter 7

Lesson 5:
The Conversion Experience

Homework, Learning, and Studying – Know Its Worth

Now that you understand how important time management is, it is time to put this into practice by figuring out your best strategy to master the work given to you in each class. Regardless of your confidence or reluctance in the course, you will need to put all your effort and dedication into the papers, quizzes, presentations, labs, and lectures. You will need to move from the simple concepts to the more complex ones to gain an understanding and produce it in the proper forum that your professors' desire.

First, it is important to show up to class physically and mentally. As simple as that seems, it is an active choice that costs. Do yourself a favor with a little math. Take your total cost and cut it in half. That is the semester cost. Divide the cost into the number of weeks. Now divide your course into the number of class meetings per week. This is the cost to you per week.

Total Cost	$25,000 divided in half
Cost per Semester	$12,500
# of weeks per Semester	15
# of classes per week	4
Cost per week	$12,500/ 15 = $833
Cost per class	$833/ 4 = $208

So, for four class meetings per week, you are paying the university this much per week and at a minimum $416 if it meets twice a week or $277 three times a week. You should have something to show for it. No refunds.

Depending on your school costs (especially if more expensive), you can see that you are wasting even more money if you do not go to class. You are still held to the same standard with the material offered in the syllabus. You need to go and maximize your financial and academic commitment. Sure, there will be days when you are sick, but most of your time should be in classes that you signed up to take. Make it a priority.

Once there, be prepared. Have your books, notes, something to write with, and a sharp mind ready to contribute to the class. Arrive early, not on time. Some professors have late policies or once the door closes, no one else is admitted. Where are you sitting? If you paid that much for a ticket to the NFL, Wimbledon, or the NCAA Final Four, you would expect to be in the front row and as close to the action as possible. Hey, treat yourself well now that you know how much you are spending.

When you were in high school, the purpose at that point was to take in the information so you could give it right back to your teacher. Now that you are in college, you need to absorb it and take on the next level of learning and understanding. You are now gaining understanding to apply it to a greater extent. Classes in your major tend to build off each other. This is why prerequisites exist. You can't take the second course without understanding the first one with a satisfactory grade.

You do this by taking notes and creating ways to keep the information relevant so you can retrieve it. Going over it constantly allows you to get to know it well. It is no different than a dancer learning a new dance routine. They go over it again and again, paying attention to every detail of the piece until it looks flawless. They do not have to think about it and just do it.

The repetition is how you demonstrate to yourself if you know the material. If you do not, this is the practice portion of the process and why starting early is best so that you have the amount of time needed to gain a true sense of the information. This is a cycle that gets repeated with all learning processes. Prepare yourself, absorb and understand the material, and create ways to remember by reviewing so that you can easily retrieve it. This repetition is taking short term information and finding ways to put it into long term memory so you can retrieve it in the manner your professors want you to give it back to them.

Study Skills

Once you understand how you process information effectively, realize that learning this skill is not a science, but an art. You will have to craft this to fit your needs. It takes time and energy to figure this out. It is not likely this will fall from the sky or happen by osmosis. Put in the work and use some trial and error to tackle this. Start by accomplishing the easy things and work toward the more complex.

Go to class. Most of what you need to know will come from this. Attendance is not enough, so immerse yourself by coming to class prepared. Take good notes. Do not write everything your professor says, try to capture the main concepts and ideas. Complete assignments and start the review process. Simply put, it will reappear soon in the form of a quiz or test. Reviewing the information will make it easier when it comes time to study for assessments. Make a note of the homework and be aware of due dates. Do the same for each class per day. When you have open time, start some of your work. You would be surprised to know how much you can get done effectively in just a little bit of time. Remember that you should study twice the number of credit hours issued - 14 credit hours = 28 hours of study time per week. If you really think about it, over the span of the week, that is about 4 hours a day - minimum. Hopefully the more you study, the greater your chances of doing well.

Study in a quiet space conducive to you being the most productive you can be. Studying in the library near the ding of the elevator and your friends spilling out can be distracting to you. Use a study carrel or a low traffic space. Minimize the distractions as best you can. Be organized and have your books, computer, etc.

Set the atmosphere for studying. Have enough lighting to see and listen to music that is conducive to studying (I prefer Jazz - It has no words and reduces out other distracting noises). Pick times to study when you are at your peak with energy. Are you a morning person or a night owl? While I do not suggest starting your studying late at night, I also do not suggest staying up all night or studying every moment of the day. There is a way to find a balance. If you have a difficult course, the best time to start is potentially right after class. The information or content is the freshest in your mind and your recall is greater. Work on tougher courses, studying them first so your energy is well spent.

Building Your Academic Muscle

How do you increase your stamina studying? The key to your success in increasing your studying time is like lifting weights. If you want to build more muscle, you would start at the strength you are capable of and incrementally increase the weights and the number of reps to build your body. Similarly, you need to start at 20-25 minutes. Focused and not distracted. Take a few minutes break and continue. As time goes on and you get more disciplined, increase the duration incrementally. A productive student should be able to study up to 60 minutes. It does not matter where you start with the amount of time to study. Get good at the process and increase your duration accordingly.

Minimize the distractions the best that you can. Put your phone away. Do not study on your bed. You will get more sleep before nighttime than in bed to rest. The two do not mix. Learn how to say no (at times) to family/friends and their wishes to hang out. It's nothing personal. Just take care of your priorities first. Trust me, their time to say no to you when they have a major assignment is coming.

Create a routine. Set start and stop times for completing studying since your schedule of classes will be different each day. Complete assignments that are due most immediately and then work on longer range assignments early so that you can pace it properly. Try and stick to that schedule as best as you can. The hardest part is simply starting to do this.

Work towards a completion goal. Say for example you want to go to the basketball game of your cross-state rival, and you have two chapters to read and a paper to offer as a final draft. Your goal is to complete the chapter readings and edit your paper PRIOR to going to the game. An incentive to keep up with your work and a reward on the other side of something you like to do, offers immediate buy-in to get everything done. You will cheer louder knowing you have accomplished the assignments and can rest easier than not doing any studying and needing to rush to complete major projects/studying. Professors can easily tell the time and effort that you put in.

7 Ps of College - Test Anxiety Cure

You are responsible with knowing a lot of information week to week over the span of a semester for each class you are taking. Professors want to know that you know what is most important. Throughout each class, there will be tests used to capture what they have offered. There is no time for freezing or being overwhelmed. You must go into them as prepared and confident as possible. Test anxiety is a term that gets tossed around by individuals as they work through the many assessments that happen over all the years you are in school. It can cause many physical, emotional, and mental symptoms for those plagued by its impact. It seems like the amount of preparation at times does not change the outcome. Students complain of being stuck in this dilemma and unable to overcome what happens to them. I do not have any clinical experience to substantiate or refute the impact of test anxiety. This is not my purpose in mentioning this as part of my narrative. Trust me, there are times I felt like I was the answer key on certain assessments. At times, I felt like I was overwhelmed and underprepared. As a student, this is going to follow you all the days of your academic life. Announced tests, pop quizzes, midterms, and finals are the ways many professors assess what you know over the course of the classes you have. Many a class will have just a midterm and a final for your overall grade. A low performance on a midterm means the pressure is on to overcome your initial test results and salvage a grade in potential jeopardy. How or what is the remedy to dealing with this properly? The answer is the 7 Ps of Being a Productive College Student: Prior, Proper, Planning, Prevents, Poor, Pitiful, Performance. I learned this from a motivational speaker. He offered this principle as he spoke to students about being scholars and not just students, and I have never forgotten it. These words, if you can apply them into your day to day habits, will make you ready for anything a professor can throw your way in the form of a question on your exams. Putting in place a plan on how to approach your studying and the kind of preparation needed to confidently prepare for tests is important. As much as we have talked about it previously, proactive preparation will build your knowledge of the material (competence) so that you are able to feel great about what you have learned (confidence) in your ability to recall the information and complete the test to the best of your ability. I am convinced that you may not have a test anxiety issue as much as you may have a deficit in preparing well for tests or quizzes. Here is a way to debunk this phenomenon and thrive in the face of adversity. After all, this is what it is all about. Let's break down the 7 Ps.

Prior - Do not wait until the last minute. Given the amount of material, you need to learn it may mean marking your calendar weeks ahead of time to begin learning the material from day one! Remember it is not just regurgitating the information. It is learning and being able to apply it. Doing a little bit at a time is a much easier haul than waiting later and needing to process so much information.

Proper - This is not just about the time factor, but also about knowing what is expected to be mastered. What kind of test is it? Is the focus on the reading, lectures, specific concepts, formulas or equations? Will the test be multiple choice, essay, true/false, or a combination? Adequate preparation means starting early enough and getting the necessary assistance from all your available resources including department tutoring, tutoring centers, individual tutors, and probably best of all, your professor and visiting their office hours. Do not delay getting the help you need. It only costs you some time and energy. Stress and anguish have no part to play in your ability to prepare confidently.

Planning - Plan your work and work your plan. It may mean you complete the reading and take notes in class. Are there any patterns or common threads that you can incorporate into how you prepare? Treat your preparation like a project manager and figure out by working from the date of the test how long it will take to complete the material. How will this prep impact this course and your other ones? Figuring out the pacing (doing something daily) and chunking (how much you do in each setting) will be an important factor in how you complete this. Some material will likely come easy to you and at times will be difficult. Again, realize the difference between homework and studying. One is to complete a task (homework) and the other is in preparation to illustrate understanding for a benchmark of your course (studying).

Prevents - You always want to put your best foot forward with all that you do. Thus, the more proactive you are in putting together a system to prepare for assessments will create habits that can be effective and repeated. The by-product of your effort minimizes your lack of preparation and increases your likelihood of mastering the information and success. So, it will mean that you seek the resources necessary to insure academic excellence. Seek the help of your professor, the students in your class, or help centers. You know if you understand the material or not. Be willing to actively seek help so you minimize not knowing how to do something. It is a sign of maturity. Getting help is a sign of STRENGTH not a WEAKNESS. Your level of preparation takes away much of the risk of not knowing something on your assessment.

Poor and Pitiful - These are coupled together because they essentially mean the same thing. Cramming or studying less than you know you are supposed to will not change the outcome. It will only be the excuse that you offer yourself in the mirror or to your peers. "I studied so hard for this. This test was so hard. I didn't know that was going to be on the test?" There are so many resources that are out there and you have no excuse for not seeking them out early and often. This is a good time to use your professor's office hours and bring to them questions that you don't understand for clarity. Ask during class, it is participation in class. You see, the kind of questions you offer in effect displays not only what you know about the concept but what they can offer to close the gap for better awareness.

Performance - You want to be the pacesetter and not be playing catch-up. Taking the right amount of time to prepare well for your classes daily will not be a heavy load to carry. Waiting five or six weeks into the semester is too late given the amount of material you may be responsible for learning. Your full-time job is as a student in preparation for the rest of your life. If this were your job and you worked for a salary, would you be demoted, fired, or promoted? Would your evaluation be, needs improvement (below average) satisfactory (average) or exceeds expectations (above average)? Raises, bonuses, and promotions go to those who outperform the standard and produce excellent work. Where do you stand and what can you do to improve your output? It is in you. Just take the time to dig deep(er).

If you can apply the 7 Ps of life to school, you can do it other important processes to manage your time. You can create habits which increase your competence in knowing the information you need to learn, thereby increasing your confidence going into any of your academic challenges. I think you don't have an anxiety problem as much as it is a preparation deficit that can be fixed by giving yourself enough time to learn new information. This process will cause you to be more organized and thoughtful with how you negotiate school.

What can you do to increase your academic prowess and incrementally prepare for all that you are faced with in a semester? As we have discussed, taking the time to read and study is a given. Now that you have managed this, I think these two practices will help you immensely. Remember the idea is to make studying simple, and not make it about how hard you study. Studying hard does not mean that you will always get it. There are some ways to make sure you can get it and work within your sweet spot.

One last tip to consider. Do not panic as you take your test. If the first few questions are not ones you know immediately, take a pause and look through other questions you may know. Sometimes you need a primer to get things started. Once you have done this, do your best. When professors write your tests, they involuntarily provide answers in other portions of the tests as well. The way they ask questions or offer potential answers in a multiple-choice test typically will give you tips for that question or inform you of an answer on another part of the test. Sometimes it also triggers what you studied or reviewed. Always eliminate the answers you know are not correct to increase your chance of picking the right response.

Learning Styles Day to Day

It is so important that you understand how you intake information and learn how to use it. We all process information differently and are good with certain subjects. It will help you to not only understand the information itself, but also how to best take in the information you are required to know. Regardless of how well you manage your time, if you are wasting time because you cannot properly attack the information so you can learn it and retain/retrieve it properly, it will be difficult to do. Remember the idea is to work smarter, not harder. The idea is to take the material from your short-term memory to a file you can retrieve in your long-term storage. Understanding how you learn will greatly help in the long run.

Here are tips for studying based on your learning style:

Auditory Learners

1. You remember what you hear so say the question/answers aloud
2. Talk while you write
3. Record yourself practicing
4. Make up songs or mnemonics and word associations

Visual Learners

1. You remember what is seen or read
2. The process of writing will increase comprehension
3. Try color coding your cards (use different inks or colored cards for dates, key concepts, theories, formulas, etc.)

Kinesthetic Learners

1. You learn by hands-on practice and imitation
2. Learn by touching doing (turning the flashcards over)
3. Incorporate movement with your learning (pacing back and forward)

Understanding which style you identify informs how you approach the process of learning the material. Nothing is foolproof and does not mitigate the difficulty of the material. What it will do is provide you with the best approach to mastering it. Control the things you can control such as how you manage your time and the manner used to study.

Your counseling or tutorial center may have these resources available for you to check out. If you are taking a college 101 type course, see if your professor can offer an inventory during class. Contact these centers in person to see if they offer an assessment or a resource online that can help you figure out which type of learner you are. It will inform your next steps and offer tips on maximizing how you learn.

Individuals tend to be strong in at least one of the three categories. You still need to incorporate the others. As an auditory learner, for example, you will still need to write down information and observe during lectures or use charts to learn. If you are practicing a speech for a presentation (visual or auditory) you may infuse movement (Kinesthetic) to show transitions as cues for the introduction, main points, or the conclusion helping you remember key components of the presentation.

Flashcards - Jack of All Trades

Whether 3x5, 4x6, any of your favorite colors, or via Quizlet and other virtual programs, the flashcard has real power in being able to assist you in learning incrementally all that may be asked of you. I think they provide a day to day opportunity to learn what is asked of you. It works fantastically with the concept I have of pacing and chunking mentioned earlier. Now you can even make flashcards electronically, so either way is fine.

There are some givens for academic success:

1. Attending class
2. Taking good notes
3. Keeping up with the reading or related assignments

It is important to not play catch up. Being behind means you must put so much emphasis on your class(es) that something invariably gets left out or you expend so much energy that it is hard to sustain this kind of effort.

My suggestion is that most of your course includes learning key theories, concepts, applications, formulas, people, events, specific related vocabulary, dates, etc. Again, it is not enough to know these data points, but how to apply them in the context of the course. Using flashcards you make or use online can help you keep track and learn this material. It will take some time but remember the key to learning this information is based on the repetition and exposure to the material. Do so chapter by chapter and bring this information to life. Flashcards have ability to help you learn several ways including the following:

- Flashcards help you retain information over the long term.
- Flashcards trigger your mind to actively recall what you need to know and store it over time.
- Flashcards force you to decide what you put on each card and how much detail is necessary to learn the information (metacognition). You decide what is priority.
- Flashcards are used to drill the information until you know it. Practice is a key element of learning.

As you read, make flashcards for key concepts. Life is full of choices, so you can do what works best for you. Making flashcards is a good study method to use on a nightly or weekly basis. Either make them for what you have read in each night or make them at the end of the week as a part of your review. When the test has been announced or seen on the syllabus, use what is called the Leitner System to prepare. Regardless of your learning style, flashcards assist you as a Visual, Kinesthetic or Auditory Learner. This system has you study the things you do not know as well until you are able to recall it all. Use this method throughout your study time during the week. Here is the process:

1. Use 3 stacks.
2. Put all your cards in one stack and review them. If you get a card right, move it to stack 2. If you get it wrong, it stays in stack 1.
3. Review stack 1. Move correct cards to stack 2 but keep incorrect cards in stack 1.
4. Review stack 1. Review stack 2. If you get a card right, move it up to stack 3. If you get it wrong, move it back to stack 1.
5. Review stack 1. Review stack 3. If you get a card right, it can leave the stack and you don't have to study it again. If you get it wrong, it goes all the way back to stack 1.
6. Repeat until you know it all.

Study Buddies - The Power of Numbers

The next is just a tried and tested strategy that gets results too. Having a study buddy really does work. I first saw international graduate students working in groups at the library when I was a freshman. The session looked like chaos and not as constructive. I was only seeing and hearing their passion for learning spoken in their native languages and not their actual effectiveness. I was not initially connected to anyone in my classes. Partly because I was shy and most importantly not wanting to be too vulnerable with what I did not know. I got over my issues, and I have used a study buddies from my sophomore year on. Since doing so, I noticed an improvement in my preparation and performance on assessments. Because I went in prepared and had done a good bit of the legwork of having materials completed, I knew more than I realized and became a "contributor" also. Study buddies increased my overall confidence and competence. My grades were proof in the pudding so to speak. Studying with productive people helps in many ways. It creates credibility and accountability to your portion of the material as well as the accountability of the other members of your group. All members of the group will help get everyone organized, productive, identify gaps in knowledge, and offer clarifying questions/answers of this material. Working in groups is a skill that you should begin to develop now. You will use it in the workforce. I guarantee it. Be prepared to contribute to group presentations in any course. Your grade will depend on your individual contribution and be a component of the final product. Nothing is worse than a person in your group not being prepared and everyone's hard work getting sabotaged because they chose to slack off and not complete the task. You do not want to be them. If you did this in your job for a major project or a key account, your boss would show you the door quickly.

Here are some tips to consider in finding committed members of a study group:

- Choose people who are serious about the work that you are doing. People who are going to distract or minimize what you are doing are going to be unproductive.
- Anyone coming to the session to just sponge the info from everyone else and not offer anything must go or step up their game and serve others in order to stay.
- Set clear mutually agreed upon expectations regarding the duration, length of session, content covered, etc.
- Everyone should be given time to offer to the group the things they know in hopes of the group mastering all the info.
- Minimize distractions like your phone. You can put your phones on silent, put them away, or stack your phones in the middle of the table.

- Environment is important. Go to a separated space or designated room in the library. You may have to reserve a location if necessary.
- Set time limits and understand everyone's obligations. Decide what you want to cover in the session.
- Create to do lists to make sure everyone stays on task.
- Include study techniques that engage everyone i.e. quiz games, flashcards, etc. You are more likely to remember more as you increase the diversity of ways you learn the information.
- As you teach, you are offering explanations of what you know. Providing the information in terms you understand and can offer to your study buddies in more broken-down terms makes it more effective than reading from your professor's notes.

While these study skills are not foolproof, I believe they create alternatives for you to use daily. Not all subjects will work perfectly, and you may just have to bear down and show some grit with learning the material on your own. I suggest experimenting to see what works and is the best way to go for you.

Chapter 8

Lesson 6:
NETWORKING

Your Go-To People

As I have suggested before, you do not always need to know the answer. It is important to know who has the answer. The number of resources available to you is countless. Many of them go unused and undervalued. There is no sense in making this more difficult than necessary. In other words, make your request known to the right person and more times than not they will address your needs. So many of the resources available are FREE. For a college student that is music to your ears and your pockets. If you need to find an internship, develop your resume and cover letter, or practice mock interviews, these services are free. If you have trouble learning subject(s) there are tutors abound on campus in many of the subject matter centers for writing, math, sciences, etc. Many of these services go under used and typically are FREE. Look for organizations to develop a skill or stronger connection to your peers (culturally, spiritually, socially, etc.) and service to others locally or globally. Yes, they are free! For example, when you graduate and start looking for jobs, resume services can total into the hundreds of dollars. Use all your resources at your institution. It is that important.

Professors

Getting the information from the horse's mouth is most important. Your professor is your absolute best resource. Office hours right before or after class are good times to speak with your professor. Asking questions about your coursework is free. Based on my own experience, a guess is that their office hours have fewer visitors until it is test time or the paper is due. While this is not a major crime by no means, remember the point is to be proactive and not reactive. In other words, consistent interactions with your professors helps you in the following ways:

- You can get your questions answered so you are clear on assignments or assessments.
- You can request feedback or clarity on assessments, papers, etc.
- You can find out how you can be most successful in their class.
- You create a level of visibility beyond the classroom.
- You learn creative or innovative ways to problem solve that may not occur during class.
- Your professors are more likely to know and remember you.
- It increases your knowledge that you can use when completing homework and studying.
- Students who take an interest in their class are potential candidates for internships, scholarships, research and other opportunities - many professors write and publish articles, books, journals, and present at conferences.
- Professor can write letters of recommendations or provide you references and contacts as you look for work and graduate programs. Beyond teaching, professors have social networks, colleagues, and

friends. A referral is an indirect way of endorsing your candidacy for great opportunities.

- They can become mentors or sponsors.
- When or if they are not available, they can suggest any additional resources on campus or in the department to use for assistance.

When you speak to your professor here are things to remember during your chat:

- Professors are human. They are not fire-breathing nor walking dictionaries only using multi-syllable words. They bleed red blood like the rest of us. Professors have wisdom and knowledge to share. This is their life's work in educating the next set of leaders.
- Come prepared with good questions. Going to your professor and simply saying, "I do not understand" does not really offer the clarity needed to address your issue. It also implies that you have not done any reading or research on the subject. Offer specific information about what may be confusing so they can pinpoint and address it properly.
- Be truthful. The dog did not eat your homework, nor did you get stuck in a blizzard in October. Honesty is going to win you more points. Trust me, professors have heard it all.
- If you get an allowance, follow through. Nothing is worse than getting an extension and not fulfilling it. You will not be able to come back. You get one blue chip to cash in, so don't waste it.
- Be concise and to the point. The office hours may be short, and you do not want to waste time.
- Stay professional. Do not let your guard down. Maintain appropriate behavior and actions. There is too much at risk for you and them.

Finally, your professors are the individuals issuing the grades they see before them. You are the person earning them. Please do not offer this phrase ever, "My professor _gave_ me a __ grade." You earn it based on your performance or lack thereof. Your professors can only grade what they see before them. If you do not complete the assignments, there is nothing to grade. The statement is misguided because it absolves you of the responsibility of doing what is required of you to complete the class successfully. Do not allow anyone to _give_ you anything. Be at no one's mercy, and take a proactive approach, managing this important relationship for every class that you are enrolled in.

Create Your Own

There are hundreds or thousands of students on campus. Do you need to know everyone? Is it even possible? Possible, yes. A necessity, no. Chances are you may know someone from your high school, city, or state that is from your area. While this is a good place to start, it is up to you to make your own way and identify the folks you want to hang with and be friends. Positive people beget positive people, and everything else in between. It is important to be friendly and open; however, picking friends is an art not a science. Whatever kind of people you want to hang with, I am sure you will find them. Be in control. As you complete the vetting process of the individuals you will call your friend, ask yourself several questions:

1. Do you know who you are?
2. What are your values?
3. What are your goals?
4. What do you have in common with them?
5. Are you more invested in the friendship than they are?
6. What are your immediate and short-term goals?
7. Are the people in your life leaders or followers?
8. Are they pouring good things in your life?
9. Does the rumor mill start or end with them?
10. Do they act differently around different sets of people?
11. Are they takers or givers?
12. What is their level of focus for school?
13. Do they make choices that fit your lifestyle or someone else's?

There are many things to consider and this can impact the trajectory of your experience. Do not take this lightly. It is important to understand that who you associate with will have the ability to influence you to mediocrity or excellence. It is true that you could say yes or no to anyone or anything. This will affect your newfound freedom. There is time for fun and there is time to get down to business. Are they a good resource and an accountability partner to you? Remember turnabout is fair play. What kind of friend are you? You must be a friend to have a friend. Someone is evaluating you also. It is likely that you will have people who are acquaintances, friends, or close friends that you confide in with your deepest thoughts. You don't want them putting you on blast. It would not be cool if they disclosed something intimate. It is not the amount of people in your circle, but it is the quality of the people in your circle that matters most. These people in your life could become your best man, godparents, and life-long friends.

Your Ladder Holders

As people, we are always seeking others to support us. The connection and accountability to another individual creates a bond that brings out the best in you. The people you surround yourself with on this journey will make or break the experience. If it does not, you may want to seek like-minded individuals to support your objectives. Here is a question to consider: do you know who the people are holding your ladder? The ladder is a metaphor for the aspirations and goals you are seeking to achieve. Some givens are that you are on a strong and stable foundation that is not going to falter when you step upon it. As you start climbing each rung of the ladder, you do so with the confidence that each step is moving you closer to the next step. You have no need to look down at what you have accomplished. Your vision is on the next rung of the ladder, making sure to work in rhythm and step with perfect timing as you reach. As you move higher, the ladder unintentionally wobbles and causes you a bit of angst. During the pause, you call out to the people below near the ladder to ask, "Hey, is everything okay? The ladder moved? Several of the people you have entrusted below say in a calm and empowering voice as they move into position, "You are good. It did move a little bit, but we got it. Keep going. We will hold it steady." Based on their reassurance, your trust in them, and your desire to reach your ultimate destination on your ladder, you continue the climb to the top. Now, would you put any random person on the side of your ladder that does not have your best interest at heart? Of course not. You only want people you know who have similar values, interests, and mutual respect as you climb the ladder of success. This is not a one-sided equation. What you put in is what you should expect to get back from them. Anything less and you are more worried about the ladder wobbling than focusing on your goals. Be willing to hold the ladder for others as they will hold it for you.

Your support system, aka "go-to people", are those individuals who you go to for sound advice and people with your best interest at heart. You had a set of "go-to people" at home. They were likely your parents, favorite teachers, trusted family members (immediate and extended), coaches and bosses. Now, you need to establish an additional set of people in your new setting. This will likely include students, student services professionals, professors, staff, and administrators. Make it a point to get to know them. Anyone saying to you, "Stop by and let me know how you are doing," is someone you should connect with because they have already laid the red carpet out for you. They clearly know what it takes to be successful and they want to see you thrive and allow you to have a pillow (someone who comforts you and allows you to blow off steam) or someone who is a pillar (advocate and resource for you to utilize in accessing specific needs). Both are necessary at the right time. Their role in your life can be significant and empowering. Be ready to build a trusting partnership and know that even if you do not like or totally agree with all that they have offered, it is meant to grow you. In building muscle, the soreness is proof that you have put in the work. These individuals happen to be building your mind for greatness that maybe they only see in you. Stay woke. You are on your own, yet you do not have to do this alone.

Administrators

As administrators and student services professionals, it is by design that they want to check on your well-being. Student retention is their role at the institution. If someone notifies them that you are not doing well in one aspect or another (grades, attendance, missing work, etc.), they will require you to meet with them. While this is not the best of circumstances, it is always in your best interest to do so. The last thing you want is for someone to throw you a lifeline when you're drowning and by not collaborating with them say, "Oh, I am fine. I am clearly drowning and see the lifeline you have thrown me." "I am okay even though I am nearing my last breath with little strength left to keep floating." Putting your pride aside will only improve your situation so you can solve your problem. Again, let them do their job so they can make your life easier.

Get Involved

Being at college and in the environment creates a lot of energy. There is so much to take in that it is quite daunting to see the sea of people moving about day in and day out. The first few days will be an eye-opening experience for you. There is no getting used to the number of people however small or large the campus is. Don't let this intimidate you. Just start in baby steps with beginning to meet your next set of friends, your next college roommate, business partner, maid of honor, best man, or godparent to your children someday. These people will be influential in the rest of your life. You cannot do this in your room. Get out. Be receptive to the many ways to meet lots of great people like yourself. Everyone is looking for similar things, so create social bonds and connect to your school so that the ties that bind you are like cables and not just strings. I have a special place in my heart and mind for James Madison University and Ball State University. They both have helped shape me into the person I am today. No denying it. I would like to think I did things to leave my mark as well. After all, we want to leave our mark (legacy) in some way. It does not have to be your name on a building or anything grand. It is about leaving a place better than you found it.

The great part about college is that now you can remake yourself. Regardless of who you have been up to this part of your life, remember that this is a clean slate for you to create an entirely new you. It may go without saying but I mean a new you that you will be proud to see in the mirror. If you were the shy one previously, it is time you find the confidence like you have never had it before to spread your wings and fly like an eagle. If you were the untamed one, then find the courage to tame a polished and refined new you. All the possibilities exist for you.

Balancing Act(s)

Find a way to balance the social against your studies, not the other way around. Focus your first few weeks on getting a full view of everything. Many organizations on campus are looking for new members. See what they have to offer, sign up or go to their meetings/events to see if they fit into your world. Remember they should fit in your world not you are fitting into them. This mistake has been costly to many a student because your intent in participating is in no way a bad thing. Focus. Focus on the reason you are there. It is to gain an education first. Yes, having fun is included in the mix also; however, if you are involved in too much, it becomes very quickly feeling like making every meeting and every event. Class, homework, studying, and being prepared is important to make sure you are off to a good start. Take baby steps. Choose a couple of things that are interesting to you and make sure they do not detract but add to your experience. Some organizations require a GPA threshold in order to become a member of them or keep active within them. Remember, you are trying to establish your GPA. Do you see how this could be counterproductive?

Once you have found the right fit for yourself, observe and see how things work and what contribution you can make to them. Maybe you are an organizer, fund-raiser, social media extraordinaire or natural born collaborator helping people come together and serve others in one capacity or another. Your part may play a key role in your organization's success. Maybe you do not see any organization that meets your needs. Well, create your own! Yes, all the organizations on campus were not there previously, but someone created them, and the groups have sustained enough momentum to be around for you to take part in them. As you move forward with your college career, keep track of the things you are part of because they will become your eventual resume`. Showing your skills and talents to get great results are what potential employers are looking for from star candidates. Start keeping track of you your progress. These day to day experiences will translate into something great for your future. Whether it is meeting some of your best friends, potential significant and influential people in your life, or like me it will become a life-long passion that has become my life's work. This was all because I exposed myself to a new experience and took advantage of it.

Chapter 9

Lesson 7:
Be Self Aware - Line in the Sand

Maslow's Hierarchy of Needs states that if you take care of basic needs, you can achieve higher needs. The kind of foundation you lay down (sand or concrete) will inform the type of structure you will be able to build. This illustration is a good visual to highlight the need to take good care of yourself so you can reach higher and higher. There are so many hours in a day and it is up to you to savor every moment. Being on either end of the extremes is not a good place to be. All work and no play or all play and no work. Let's face it, college can be a challenging environment. The demand, rigor, and volume of work has a cadence all its own. As you ride this wave of work, it is important that you run this and not let it run (ruin) you.

You do this by giving your body a chance to rest or let off steam. Provide your mind with a needed and well-deserved break. For as often as you need to be up and ready to produce, you need to make time to have some "me" time. What do you like to do? Is it playing basketball, tennis, working out in an aerobics class, painting, playing guitar, cooking, community service, or other thousands of choices? These things you should take time to do also. You will need to incorporate them into your schedule, so they provide you with a needed safety-valve, so you are able to rejuvenate and decompress. Some of the most successful people I know have stated, "I will know I am in a good place when I am able to workout at least 3 times per week." I think it is important to work and work diligently over the week; however, it does not mean 7 days a week and 24 hours a day. You would not last a semester like this. I am suggesting the following formula for maximizing the most out of the most precious commodity you own, you:

- Take a moment and unplug for 30 to 60 minutes a day with no social media. This is the way it used to be for many of us. Silence your phone and "TTYL".
- Eliminate nay-sayers and negative people from your phone, social accounts, and life.
- Put positive affirmations on your mirror or on your screen savers to remind you how great you are, even if you are a work in progress.
- Dress to impress on test days - you will feel more confident going into your exams.
- Keep your room and desk clear and clean.
- Eat your meals, get a proper amount of rest, and always make time for yourself.
- Talk to professional counselors and sort through your unresolved issues. It is free.
- Take a long shower or bath and wear your favorite robe to relax. If you don't have one, get one.
- Have your own spa day!! Pedi, Facial, Mani (why not all) I am sure you could find others to do this with at least monthly.
- Try stretching, exercising, long walks, and sweat.
- Eat well and minimize the junk food.
- Take a 15 to 20 minutes power nap once a day. They help reduce your sleep debt.

- Choose one day of the week that is yours when you do no homework.
- Take daily breaks and keep your energy up.
- Meditate or do yoga and deep breathing.
- Listen to natural sounds like a beach, creek, forest, pond, lake, etc.

Once you have your self-care ritual, go for the higher needs by doing this:

1. Establish a schedule and create it with some consistency throughout the week.
2. Follow your schedule the best as you can and take care of your academic and job responsibilities.
3. Set and establish a consistent study schedule (number of credit hours x 2) per week.
4. Have start and stopping times to study.
5. Spread your study hours over the span of the week. Studying during the day is okay too.
6. Work 6 days a week. Remember even God rested on the 7th day.
7. Work in increments that allow you to focus and get things done, starting at 25 to 30 minutes; then, increase it until you to reach a full hour of studying.
8. Incorporate exercise or other physical activity into your day.
9. Create a bedtime ritual for yourself so that you can wind down from the day
10. Set and keep a stop time for yourself studying nightly.
11. Use school activities as an incentive to get things done so you can attend them and enjoy - read two chapters for class before you go to the game, dance, bowling, intramurals, etc.
12. Repeat 1 to 12 weekly and watch your academic progress improve.

It may seem like a lot to handle. Imagine what it would be like if you do not have any self-care habits for yourself. Chaos and burning the candle from 3 ends is not the answer. Take the time to make it happen. The results will provide you the balance, rest, repeatable positive habits, fun, and a well-deserved rest from the books. It is not a request. It is a requirement.

Leader in the making

Consider this. If knowledge were water, are you a sponge or a rock? Be able to answer this question at any point when you are facing a challenge and make the choice to absorb what is being offered and not let it pour off you. Depending on where you are in life, the chance to absorb the knowledge (water) may only happen once. "I finally did it, and now my life will never be the same." As you chart your legacy from this point on, I want you to be able to offer the same comment to someone one day when they ask you this question. You can only offer your testimony, once you have passed your test.

Building Off of Successes and Failures

The moment you are born, you are dependent on someone to care for and nurture you. Whether being nursed, bottle fed, having your diaper changed, being cared for when you are sick, and crying or just needing to be held and soothed, you do not know how to do anything. Instinct may have helped you crawl, yet someone helped you to stand and walk. Someone helped you with the transition from the bottle to sippy cup and learning to be potty trained. It was not easy and at times not even fun. At times you may have fought tooth and nail, but all of it needed to happen in order to be able to take care of yourself. Additional advances included dressing yourself, learning your letters, and how to read and compute. The list goes on and on.

Along the way, some things came easy for you and others may have been difficult. Ask your parents to offer you story after story about your history. It did not minimize the desire for these things to happen and each success meant that another goal of one sort or another was placed before you. It needed to be known, practiced, and done to the best of your ability until you got the hang of the new task. There were failures too. We have all had them and we have some battle scars from our bouts. We lose sight of them because success is always the goal. We do not have to be perfect at what we do, but excellence is a better level of achievement. Nothing in life including all of us is perfect. It is not necessary. The motive is to do your best given all the knowledge and resources accessible to you.

With this said and now in the present, college is no different of an experience. You do not have to possess all the answers (perfection), but you do need to know how/where to find the answers and apply it to your life (excellence). This four-year journey requires you to be comfortable with being uncomfortable at times. By this I mean you don't know what you don't know. Your quest day in and day out is to find the answers to all the questions you have, and the ones posed to you. Your entire experience will be preparing yourself to search and find out as much as you possibly can.

Michael Jordan, one of the most famous athletes in the world, had his own journey. Cut as a sophomore from his basketball high school team, he worked hard and became the athlete we have known him to be. A famous quote from him that sticks with me is, "You miss all the shots you never take." Failure is a fact of life, it does not define you and when used properly, it will propel you to success. This does not mean you do not prepare for tests or write great papers. It does mean tapping into all the knowledge available to present your best self. Give yourself a chance to fail to accomplish more. Be on a quest to do your best seeking excellence, not perfection. Simply put, we are not perfect, and you do not have to be.

Chapter 10

Lesson 8:
My Odyssey

My illustration is not the gold standard. It is filled with mistakes and milestones that I own, and it worked for me. As an average Joe, mediocracy had gotten me but so far and here is how I got to where I stand now attempting to impart some knowledge your way now. Trust me when I say if I can turn it around, I know with the same grit you can do the same.

Rocky Start

My freshman year again started with me not really knowing what I was doing or how to even do it. Thank goodness I went to class, but much beyond that I did the minimum academically and lived my social life to the fullest. Ironically, I went home for a weekend in the early part of my freshman year. Upon my return, guys on my floor were patting me on the back and congratulating me. As a ploy, they made me the floor representative for the Hall Council in my residence hall. I did not really know what that meant and upon a little more sleuthing, found out I attended meetings and represented concerns and ideas of the guys on my floor. It seemed simple enough. Go to a meeting and work with other reps and Hall Directors. With my second term underway and my lackluster GPA, I decided to begin to buckle down, some. Things were better and I began to manage my time a little better and study more. I began to get the kind of results that allowed me to improve but not much beyond this. With me injuring my foot in the third term, it provided me the necessary time and effort to begin to see the glimpses of my abilities that I needed to see moving forward.

What I soon learned and is a valuable lesson for you is the first semesters lay down the foundation for what will become your GPA. The better you do in the early stages, the easier it is to build or sustain. The lower your GPA starts, the harder it is to bring it up. The reason is that you are now working against the cumulative number of credit hours you have taken. With improvement to your grade point, the "jump" is typically minimal. Here is what I mean. If your overall average is a 2.5 out of 4.0 with a total of 50 credit hours taken and you raise your GPA for a semester to 3.0 with 15 hours, although an improvement, it may raise your overall GPA incrementally. It is harder to raise your GPA after 65 credit hours (50 + 15) and the improvement must be substantial. Over the span of my undergraduate college career, I went from a 2.1 to a 2.89. In that time, I had several semesters when I had a 3.0 GPA or better and it never came close to being over 3.0 overall. I learned this lesson too late.

The Comeback

During my sophomore year, I came back with a renewed commitment to my academics. After discussions with my parents over the summer, I knew I could do more and so did they. The plan for my year was to assume a role as Vice President of the Hall Council. I previously served as a floor representative with another student serving as President.

84

Upon my arrival to school, a lot had changed to say the least. A lot of my running buddies at school did not return due to low grades or lack of desire. The President did not return because of a family illness that impacted her financially. So now I was thrusted into the leader as President. "Uhhhh, I am not ready!" I thought. With the help of my Hall Directors, I figured out how to make it work. This term was about to be up to this point my heaviest load of courses. I befriended some cool new friends who reintroduced me to Jazz music. My parents, especially my dad, had listened to it and I was exposed but never considered it a medium I would enjoy. There was too much to listen to like Rap and R&B which I loved. The difference being, I used mellow Jazz to study with because it had no words and helped me focus on my reading and studying. We kind of adopted each other. For the first time, I employed different study methods and adapted my days to get work done. I used times between classes to read, review, rewrite, or recite something. I began to make my study ritual at night more manageable. I took power naps when I felt myself getting tired and needing to take the tired bug edge off. 15 to 30 minutes was all it would take. I ate dinner, watched the news until about 7 pm, and went into my study cocoon until about 11:30 every night. I started studying in increments of about 30 minutes and increased it to nearly an hour straight without a break. I made myself a "Things I Gotta Do" list to track my progress, see my schedule for the following day, and track all I needed to complete. When the study lounge or my room were too noisy, I either turned the Jazz up enough to drown it out or started hanging at the library in the study desks. I was still too social to be distracted by all the people I had gotten to know out on my own. My US History class was my first venture into using study buddies for tests. I loved History and had a knack for the info. As we studied together, I realized how much I knew and was able to rattle off answers to questions and both teach and learn. My memory was vivid with the info. I soon learned to translate this process into my other courses. It netted my first 3.0 GPA. While it may not be a great feat for some, it was my first and I could not have been prouder to open my report card in front of my parents over the next few terms. Even though I did not maintain a 3.0 over my entire year, I had figured out the art of studying. Now, I was on repeat mode. Meanwhile, as President of my Hall Council, I was now exposed to other parts of the university that I did not know existed or understood how they fit into the bigger picture of impacting everyone's experience. I was invited to receptions and dinners with administrators and influencers. A friend of mine told me about the possibility of becoming a Resident Assistant. It required you to take a prerequisite course for 6 weeks. I did it and went through the process of becoming an RA. I became one and it required me to move out of my residence into another part of campus, and it came with an ability to influence the experience and exposure to college life.

Cruising Altitude

As a junior, I went back early because I was training as a Resident Assistant and learning the ropes of how to do this new role that provided me the resources to serve others and impact the culture of the hall I worked and the university. It also was like a scholarship, of sorts. You see by being an RA, the university waived my room and board costs as part of my college costs - tuition only. The only way to lose this was by being let go from your role because of a poor performance or a violation being broken in the role. By now, I had a good sense of how to study and was able to make sense of it all. This was great because the demand was greater in my major classes and my new role. Even more important for me was to be diligent and true to the study patterns I had established the previous year. I needed to call a couple of audibles to succeed even more. The first was not being so visible when I was not on duty. In the role, if you see a violation, it is your responsibility to confront the person/issue. Sometimes this could take seconds and other times hours. I was not avoiding anything, but I still had and held my priorities academically. I used my idle hours more effectively and changed my location to study in the 24-hour lounge of the library. I saw and heard great things about being there and used it several days out of the week, especially weekends. I also provided myself with incentives to stay active in college life. If I wanted to go to a dance, party, games, play ball, intramurals, and go off campus to a buddy's spot to get away from it all, I had to get work done so that I could enjoy, relax, and not have my work looking over my shoulder. Many times, I was successful, and only a few times did this backfire on me and impact my grades. What I came to learn was that I needed to be even more prepared and anticipate other's missteps. My demanding schedule required me to keep my to-do list even more closely managed. My grades did not suffer and because I was busier, it meant that I had to manage myself more and it seemed like I got so much more done. I'm not sure if it is mind games or reality. I chose me finally and was operating at full strength.

Apex

In my senior year, still being an RA in the same hall previously assigned, many of the Hall Directors I knew asked me about next steps and what was in my future. I remember them saying, "Reg are you interested in a master's degree in College Student Personnel Administration?" At the time I thought to myself, "I don't want to be a Hall Director?" This in no way casting negativity on the role, I was simply not aware of all that life had to offer me and only saw this through a very limited scope. Little did I know about life at the time. As I neared my final curtain call, the realization that this was almost over and I was about to move on to greener pastures was when I took my senior portrait early fall. As I literally reached in my closet to grab my grey suit and red and grey tie, I realize I would not be walking these halls again. My dose of reality was even greater that I needed to do even more when I had a candid conversation with my academic advisor. As I went to check in to see what was outstanding and confirm that my prior pacing of previous terms was going to net graduation, I asked my advisor about the prospect of graduation and the following question, "What would I be able to do with a Political Science degree?" My adviser without hesitation said honestly, "I do not know!" Much to my surprise, I naively thought that he was not doing his job and what was he good for? Well the answer to that question was within me, so the real question became, "What are YOU going to do?" It was time to put my cumulative experience into a neat and visible package and finish as strong as I could. The Black Student Association President asked if I would serve on the Executive Board and I agreed. There was plenty on my plate and it meant the same thing, studying hard, playing some and managing all that I agreed to do. In the middle of my winter term, I was asked to volunteer and go on an admission yield trip as a student ambassador. It meant meeting potential students and parents and answering questions about my experience as a student at Ball State. Again, I thought easy enough and I went. Families came to the reception site and I along with others mingled and chatted about college life. It was instinctual and exciting to me. I was engaged and able to answer based on my Residence Life experience and exposure to all the resources on campus that I helped students with day to day. Sidebar conversations about other aspects of college life pulled many families in and was seemingly able to convert unsure students to new Cardinals. I was asked to do another trip and did. The same results occurred. A couple of administrators asked if I had thought about working in the Admissions Office and the thought had never crossed my mind. I took it under serious consideration as I thought about the question I posed to my adviser.

With some renewed vigor and passion, I followed up with a member of the Admissions team to learn more. The more I learned the more it seemed like a good fit for me. My Hall Director offered to help me pull together a resume of my previous experiences, and a few hours later had my first resume ready to offer.

I was in my last term and needed to take an overload to graduate on time. It was 18 credit hours and included an internship. Never had I taken more than the allowable threshold (16 hours). Keeping all the plates spinning was a lot to handle. What I came to learn about myself was that I was capable of so much more as a young adult. That 17-year-old naive young man had turned a corner in a way that I did not expect. I did not know that I had the capacity to achieve a few years earlier. I chose to make the decision to simply try and do better. Oh, by the way, I finished the term with my highest-grade point average for one term a 3.55! Was I smart, a hard worker, or fortunate? I think all three are true. If you would have told me this, I would have laughed or clearly not seen this coming.

As one of 60 applicants for a position in the Admissions Office, I was granted an interview and officially offered the job in June. With a final internship and elective completed over the summer, I had my first job in July prior to graduation which happened a month later. I am still beyond words when I think about it. This happens to other people, not someone like me. My higher education career began as a cumulative series of events that I could not have predicted or imagined.

Passion Found – Higher Ed

Ironically, the first assignments I had in my job as an Admissions Counselor was to welcome families during Orientation and have dinner with parents. My conversations invariably ended up talking about how I managed my college life with all that it entailed. As I talked with them, I felt like every word I offered they clung to so they could offer advice to their students.

As a new professional in a brand-new world, it was now my role to pay it forward to as many students as I possibly could by helping them get into college. Although my role was seemingly limited, I was not any the wiser and attempted to do what I could to do my job and serve others. I learned my job and did it to the best of my ability. I traveled to high schools in the region, making presentations to students and informing counselors of changes or improvements at the university. Once they applied, I reviewed their applications and offered a decision among the committee members. I got a chance to see parts of the state and region I had never seen before. I met colleagues who did similar roles and other universities. I discovered my ability to influence students and offer information that made Ball State competitive and relevant. One student who stood out to me among many was a young lady I assisted with getting into the school. She and her parents came to my office during their visit and talked about her situation. Ball State was her school because we had her specific major, Speech Pathology. Her grades were not great, and she just wanted a chance to prove herself. In hearing her story, I felt like I wanted to go to bat for her and advocate for her getting into school. I knew a young man like her that needed support to get to the other side. It was my last day at Ball State and felt like I had come full circle advocating for her admission.

Empathy and Serving

I did this role for two years and went to Butler University in Indianapolis as an Assistant Director in charge of recruiting and selecting students of color for a full scholarship. I traveled far and wide in the US searching for the brightest and most talented. The amount of influence I had was even greater now because I had more resources to offer and an ability to help make it happen. There was one student I met at a College Fair in Chicago. He was poised and offered a challenge to me in understanding what made my school so special verses the institutions he was also considering mostly Big Ten Schools. Our casual conversation carried on for several minutes and he filled out some info for me to stay in touch. Somehow my counselor's hat was put back on like it was at Ball State with the young woman. I remembered him and felt compelled to check on him. I followed up with a phone call several months later and we picked up from where we left off. He had not applied yet and the deadline was slowly approaching. He was playing on his high school baseball team and had practices that would prevent him from coming for an interview as part of the process. My comment to him was, "Are you willing to throw a full scholarship down the drain?" The question convinced him to drive to Indianapolis and speak to the scholarship committee I co-chaired on a Sunday morning. The interview went amazing and the committee was wowed by his academics, charm, and charisma. He got the scholarship to attend Butler University and changed the trajectory of his life. My innate skills helped draw this student out of their comfort zone and take a calculated risk. Paul, thank you for believing in me and the process.

Fork in the Road

Helping students was just a natural progression. It was not enough just to get them admitted into the school I worked. It was important that they keep in touch once they got there to make me aware of their progress or concerns. Unfortunately, it became a game of hit and miss. Between my travel schedule and their courses and breaks, not much got accomplished. It felt weird to get them in and not be able to see them through to the very end. I needed a position that would allow me to impact in that way. A role at Allegheny College became available and I put my name in the hat for it. The role was Director of Multicultural Affairs and a step up but a huge undertaking. Now I would get the chance to use my passion and help even more students from matriculation to graduation. The next few years was about establishing myself as a professional capable of changing chaos to completion. We talked out the process one on one and helped them achieve at their full potential. Like a good doctor, there were few patients that I was not able to help them climb their own individual mountain and graduate. I developed a reputation that spread to other students and improved retention and graduation rates of students of color.

Despite my ability to make a difference in the lives of students I worked with over the years, I sort of forgot about me in the grand scheme of things. I took some students to a great leadership conference in Virginia. In attending this conference and among many great speakers, one stood out and changed my trajectory. Reverend Al Sharpton was a keynote speaker and said a prophetic statement to me that is etched in my mind to this day. In speaking about leaders, he offered the following, "Leaders do a good job of taking care of others, and in the process, forget about themselves. Who takes care of leaders?" It felt like a ton of bricks fell from the ceiling and instead of speaking to the many students in the room, we were having a one on one conversation. In that moment, I realized my next step was to combine my passion of helping students and my dedication to myself even more. Up to that point, I saw the equation as one or the other, not both. It took me a minute to get there, but I had arrived at this specific crossroad. The next step for me had to be a master's and seeking more for myself. As a selfless person, it was time in a positive way to be selfish and take the natural progression of getting the proper credentials and leaving no stone unturned. A conversation with a friend about my next step followed, and she mentioned a friend she had who was looking for students to pursue a Masters in Higher Education College Student Personnel Administration. I was introduced to him and showed him my resume and was encouraged to apply. Excited and given a boost, I applied and got into a master's program with an assistantship, a stipend, and a chance to become more than I was before.

The "Graduate" Student

I moved from Pennsylvania to Virginia and was now in a master's program at James Madison University - College Student Personnel Administration. I was gaining an education and pragmatic exposure that would allow me to work effectively with college students as they embarked on their college experience. Great! I resigned from my job and went in full throttle with no lifeline. It was simple. Either sink or graduate. In my life, I had achieved a 3.0 grade point average a few times. What would it take to "maintain" an average high enough to stay? I had the professional experience of over 7 years, but no experience getting an advanced degree. At least in my mind, the Imposter Syndrome had traveled from a deep dark corner, stepped to my door, and knocked hard on my door requesting to be let into my mind. Imposter Syndrome again happens when you are among your peers and while you have met all the standards allowing you to be there, you are in a constant state of doubt and question your skills, talents, and abilities. All the while seeing yourself as an unequal. I clearly needed to shake this mindset or go down crashing and burning. I overthought the situation and went in over prepared, yet still doubted myself. There is a quote that I was living out in a horrible way: "Don't doubt your power, or you will give power to your doubt. "It finally took my girlfriend at the time (now wife, Kim, 23 years later and counting) plus good friends) to talk me off the ledge. The secret to my success was to relax more and let the classes take their natural course - read, prepare, study, and perform. Mondays, Wednesdays, and Friday from 12 to 1:30, I played ball with the fellas, talked trash, and had a great time. It was the perfect break I needed to decompress. A few weeks later with a grade or two under my belt did I finally see myself as equal as and greater than I professed myself to be. While a daunting set of circumstances I faced, I managed well above a 3.0 (a cliché that I heard as an undergrad was "3.0 or you GO," which was playing like a recording in my head). My second and third semesters of graduate school were much more like I expected and needed them to be. The last challenge I faced was my comprehensive exams and the beginning of my job search process to return to my work life. It was the cumulative total of what I learned over my time in the program. It took a lot to prepare and my study buddies were an integral part of my preparation. Only a few edits and follow up were necessary to complete my last hurdle. I was in the zone and at my best and had the grades to show for it. Two years later and using the same practices in my undergraduate degree, it paid off to get my work done, maximizing my potential. I finished the degree with a 3.63 GPA and had as high as a 3.8 in a semester during my program.

Chapter 11

Lesson 9:
The Professional Life

Perfecting My Craft and Passion

My job search was not as eventful as I thought it might be given my previous experience and now holding a Masters. I did get a few nods during a job convention I attended, but no real bites. I continued to look and came across an ad for a Director of Multicultural Affairs, but I did not really pay attention to the name of the school as much as the position itself. It sounded like me and what I was looking for. I saw the ad a few weeks earlier and realized I needed to fax my cover letter and resume for consideration. I faxed it on the deadline Friday and got a call on Monday. After a lengthy phone interview and in person meeting, I had landed the job at Cornell University in The College of Architecture, Art, and Planning. As I told classmates and mentors, I got a "Whoa" response. I was happy for their well wishes but did not understand what it meant to be at an Ivy League school.

Laid to Rest

Despite all my preparation and previous experience, I faced a bit of an "imposter syndrome," again; not as a student, but as a professional. I thought I had checked all the boxes now and thought to myself, "With the caliber of students at an institution like this who are all valedictorians and "answer keys" in their own right, what can I possibly teach these students that they do not know already or can read in a book?" I was immediately going to be put to the test because my point of entry at Cornell University College of AAP was leading students through a six-weeks program as they began their Pre-Freshman Summer Program. The idea being that this would serve as a transition program for students of color to use the summer as a springboard to the fall. It was paid for and attendance was required based on the Admissions Committee on which I served. Successful completion meant a continuation in the program and confidence towards graduation. I met my first cohort of students who came from far and wide: New York City, Los Angeles, Massachusetts, Chicago, and Texas to name a few. As I soon learned upon their arrival, it was clear to me immediately. As smart as they are and well- schooled as they have been, something clear and obvious was that they were only young adults and teenagers! My level of experience paled in comparison to anything they could tell me about life, and that was clear to me after some initial conversations and observations. So, I returned to my bread and butter as I approached the weekly seminars. I needed to present to them on preparation for their summer classes and life as a student in the fall, managing your time, setting priorities, learning when to say "no" and managing the adult decisions you need to make. As I learned that students were having academic difficulties, one-on-one sessions created trust and accountability that helped them get over the hump time and time again. I became a retention guru by helping students help themselves at one of the top universities in the country. Students who knew others were struggling would mention my name as a personal testimony to go and get help getting through school. Not only did students in my college seek me out, so did students in other colleges at Cornell University. It was an honor and privilege to serve in this capacity. This is not what I sought, but I was working within my gift.

Fly Eagle Fly

I had reached a point where I needed to call an audible. Despite my skills and abilities to do my work and do it well, my level of advancement was not happening. My role within Multicultural Affairs seemed like it did not have the level of depth perceived by the greater world to display the transferability of skills to do greater things and increase my capacity for growth. As complex and meaningful as the role in this vein of student services was, I had begun to feel pigeon-holed. As I applied for new jobs to expand my growth, my skills seem to only dictate no capacity to do more. It meant finding a role to do what I had been doing and having a more global role to display it for all to see. I took a dove tail and worked in the K-12 world and further honed my skills. I became an Assistant Dean at a Day/Boarding School and later a Director of Guidance at an Independent School. Both positions included teaching classes on Wellness. It included units on academic readiness and college preparation which was right up my alley given all my previous experience in working at colleges. As the Director of Guidance, my role was teaching and assisting students with the day to day tasks of becoming better students in school. Counseling students on social, academic, and personal matters weaved a greater web of ability to engage students to aid their progress. I was a key administrator offering insight into the trends, obstacles, and strategies affecting the student experience. Thus, able to offer programs and changes to increase student retention which was a major element of keeping capacity at tuition driven academies. Again, I was able to do this successfully and now as a trained teacher/facilitator, I developed lessons to meet the demand and increase the buy-in of it not just being my work, but the work of everyone.

After this experience, I found my way back to higher education. I took a little longer than I expected, and in the process acquired many skills that I was able to transfer into my initial position and further in my current role. It took me longer than I anticipated yet everything lined up so properly. The coaching skills I acquired allowed me to probe and not pry in the lives of my students understanding the fullness of their lives. It happened to be that I was supporting masters and doctorate students at The University of Southern California. It is one of the most reputable institutions and leader in the field of Education in the country. As a kid living in Oregon, it was my favorite school and no longer a dream but reality that I worked with their student body online. I never anticipated or expected I would find myself in this position given all my prior experience. Online? Yes, online! I had been in professional roles in higher education on the front lines with students on campus and now needed to reach them virtually. It meant the phone or live video, neither of which I had used exclusively in a job before. All of it seemed daunting working for an education technology business, yet I trusted my instincts and all my experience this time with no fear or second guessing. It paid off. The coaching training, I completed reinforced a lot of what I was already doing to make connections. I was just using a different method to do the same process of supporting students and creating relationships.

The Final Piece

My daughter was attending a local community college in the area as part of her process to transfer to a 4-year school. I accompanied her there for support, guidance, and insight. In the process of several conversations as she was working with a counselor (this counselor was instrumental in my daughter being able to transfer successfully to her four year institution), I learned the individual helping her was from JMU and attended as an undergraduate and received her Master's degree in my graduate program – College Student Personnel Administration. Ironically enough, we were there the same time! With this new connection and affiliation, I asked about roles or positions there and how to get my foot in the door. The suggestion was given to teach a College Student Development course offered to students. Yes, I became a professor and now teach a subject that I am extremely passionate about, helping students make the smoothest transition possible as they make their way to the four-year school of their choice or to productive employment. After applying and training, I started teaching a few months later. I am fortunate to be operating within my gift. As you can see, it was not easy or apparent. Roles you are in sometimes draw this out of you. Sometimes you just know. I guess mine was a hybrid. All of this was informed by a decision I made to just try and increase my ability to get better grades. There was no way for me to be able to predict the many lives I have touched and the many people that have poured into me; an 18-year-old kid from a small town in the Midwest. I'm still trying to wrap my arms around this, but I have embraced it fully now.

Chapter 12

Lesson 10:
Passing the Baton

As I see the full picture of what I experienced now, it is amazing to see my evolution from where I started to where I am now. I do not think my story is an exclusive one. It is my story, and I own it. What I learned along the way has been so much more than I could have realized. Service to others is really for me where all the intersections meet. I have always been the one, so to speak, to be approached by others and hear their problems. In hearing what they have said, I have been able to provide clarity to their issues and offer reasonable solutions that make sense or at least allow them to reflect on the impact of the choices before them and the possible consequences of their actions and behaviors. As a teenager, I thought my gift was going to be a lawyer who dressed in fancy suits, drove fast cars, and had a pretty house on a hill due to my ability to impact proper interpretations of the law and save all mankind. The gift I was granted was, as I heard a professor put it, "Answering questions but also questioning answers." I did get to dress professionally, I did not practice law, and in my own way I created access to individuals striving to make a better life for themselves and those close to them. The lessons and strategies I have offered help mold people who did not have direction into successful, driven, results-focused professionals that carry this lesson with them wherever they go in life. Many of my students have thanked me for the difference I have made in their life and their ability to emerge better than when they started on this journey called life. The tools given have helped them carve their own masterpiece using the same age-old tools, techniques, and strategies that I used and borrowed from so many before me along the way. You are on your own and should not do this alone - create your network and sphere of influence. Remember you are your institution's client and ambassador that illustrates to all you encounter how to successfully maneuver through this process. This process done properly brings you to the right conclusions and informs how you approach and engage the world through a different prism. Ultimately, you gain confidence in your abilities and this is what the world sees when they see you in action and in thought. You cannot put a price tag on this feeling of being liberated and empowered to be the best you possible. It does not mean you won't have challenges. It just means how you work through it is from a more informed space.

Oz

In some successive conversations I have had with friends and colleagues, I was imparted with some wisdom I had never considered until I began penning this guide. We all remember the movie *The Wizard of Oz*. I want to focus on the overriding theme of the movie because it speaks to this journey you are about to undertake. The Scarecrow, Lion, Tinman and Dorothy were all seeking a specific trait they felt they were lacking - imposter syndrome. The movie depicts their journey in song and at the time was considered an extraordinary movie. The Wizard, as you know, had them bring back the broom of the dead witch in order to be granted a heart, intelligence, courage and returned to Kansas. Once the curtain was pulled back, it was clear they had been tricked into their deed. Despite the Wizard's underhanded scheme and their allegiance to doing it, the Wizard provided symbolic trinkets to all of them illustrating their newfound talents or skills. After offering them each of their gifts, each of them learned the following from his specific comments about what he granted them: Each possessed the innate traits they were seeking, the journey they took in finding courage, intelligence, compassion, and "home" was already within them. The tests each of them prepared for and successfully completed confirmed the traits and feelings that they had all the time. They had now applied them in their daily life to reach their goal. My friend, you too have the skills to successfully complete this next journey of making your college experience attainable and achieving a degree. No one is going to make you bring a token to a wizard and grant your wish. You will need to dig deep and define your purpose and refine the very skills used to accomplish achieving goals, your high school diploma or Associates degree in order to get a bachelor's degree and beyond. This guide is your template to making that happen. It may work differently for each of you and that is okay. It is not meant to be the same. Write your own formula and script, minimize the bloopers, and get your reward for working smart during this next phase of life.

Technology vs. Old Fashioned

As I continue to reflect, the playing field for you and I are very different. When I attended college, there were dot matrix printers on large scrolls of printer paper and computer stations which took up a full room. Microfiche was how volumes of journals or books were kept in the library. Word processors were just beginning to replace the typewriters (manual and computerized) among many other "advances in technology." By the time I was in graduate school, email was just coming of age and the internet was just a toddler. Even Student ID cards were now holding information on them and granting you access to the dining hall and holding money on your account to take care of incidentals at the Bookstore or campus retail stores and granting entrance to athletic events. Now, your world has instantaneous access to most things and there is little to no wait for what you are looking for as you live your life with access to a global society. It is daunting to think and see all the advances in technology which in a lot of ways have made life simple, easy and has made everything at your fingertips. With the integration of technology in our daily life, it is nearly impossible to be without it for too long and it not impact you.

Yet, with all the access to the mega amount of information you have, it has not resolved one key issue that I have been talking about from the very beginning. It has not substituted for you learning how to learn. You still must do this process - the old school way. Sitting down and reading the chapters, going to lectures, understanding theories, concepts, formulas, definitions and other critical thinking skills. There are no corners to cut or instant newfound processes to make preparation for tests, quizzes, presentations, and similar assessments easier. For all the advances, many colleges and universities still have less than perfect retention and graduation rates for their clientele. Every student who goes to school is not guaranteed a college degree. Putting these previously mentioned practices into your arsenal is not a guarantee either. What it does give you is a fighting chance and an opportunity to fulfill realistic or even lofty dreams of what success looks like to you. Therefore, earlier in the guide we talked about building on your successes. It has its own cause and effect. As you rise to the challenges you have faced since you set foot on earth, you have been in constant mode of not knowing anything or how to do it and figuring it out (how to hold your head up as a baby to walking, talking, and reading, etc.). Your desire to please coupled with the support of many influential people pouring into your life has allowed you to emerge capable, competent, and confident in your current skills and talents. In this next phase you are pursuing as a student, you should look back to those previous challenges and see the process now from a prism of how I overcame and surpassed my self-doubt to complete a specific task and reach my goal. This will increase your capacity to build on your success and approach each new challenge with even more vigor to use your prior skills and talents to master the next and so on. It will take that same vigor and acquiring more skills to meet the new demands. Prior to college, I had never worked so hard on anything really. Most of what I was able to do came easy to me. I did possess the ability to push through my challenge, but never saw the need to excel. I never used the "muscle" of maximizing my potential. Not because people did not see it in me, but I did not see it in myself. Once I did put in the time and effort and saw what I could do, I faced personal and professional challenges with an "I can" attitude.

My desire for you reading this book is that you will be able to glean all the wisdom, knowledge, and strategies offered to make a difference in your process as a student. Do not make the same mistakes or fall into the same pitfalls I did. I, like you, were admonished to keep my eyes open to this but did not always heed the signs until it was too late. It will help inform your experiences as a life-long learner. Enter new this season of your life in a mutually agreed partnership with your current educational institution. Be present and open to working with your partner. As the client, remember to make your needs known and be willing to write your blueprint for how you want the world to see you. Put in the hard work to make it happen. Act with intention, and do not just react. Not doing anything is an action also. Do not be idle or passive in the process. You would not want them to be any less than eager. Remember, you are the owner of your destiny, and you do not have to do this alone; it is the relationships which makes the difference in the experience. Carve your masterpiece in conjunction with your professors, teachers, administrators, parents, mentors and peers. Work with anyone willing to help you live your (dreams) best life. Approach each encounter with an open hand, mind, and heart because you will gain so much more.

Reach

As a middle school student, I ran track and was an okay sprinter. In high school, I eventually ran the 800, 1600, and 3200 meter runs along with Cross Country. I was a decent runner and among the top in each race. The event that I loved to see but never ran was the sprint relays. The speed and timing of the race was electric and exciting. Typically, track meets came down to these events determining the meet winner. These events are especially exciting during The Olympics. The level of preparation is immense and there is so much at stake, being the fastest in the world, earning the Gold Medal and all that comes with it - endorsements, stardom, and bragging rights for the next four years.

There are only special people who dare take this on and do so at the risk of injury, disqualification, and underperforming. The secret to this race is being fast enough to establish a lead and the all-important passing of the baton to the next runner. The exchange of the baton has many nuances to a successful pass. It includes maintaining the initial runner's speed. Once the first runner reaches the mark laid out on the track, the next runner must listen for the sound of their approach and begin to sprint as well. You are given a zone of a few meters to make this all-important exchange of the baton. The runner with the baton in hand while in the specific zone must pass the baton, yells to the next runner "reach!" The next runner starts their initial sprint and without looking back puts their arm back with their hand extended to feel for the end of the baton to be placed into their hand. Once the baton is grasped out of the air, they take off as fast as they can to the next runner and the same baton pass is repeated with perfect timing and the command, "reach" being offered until they finish the race as fast as possible.

The hardest part of the relay is the baton exchange. If done outside of the zone - you are disqualified, if you drop the baton - you are done, and if you obstruct another team from their exchange being in their lane, yeah, you guessed it, disqualified. It can look like chaos to poetry in motion. The runners must know their strengths, trust their instincts, trust others, respond actively to the word, "reach;" and without looking back, know that what is being offered to them is in fact what they need to continue the race and compete to the best of their ability.

I have run this higher education race and, in the process, learned a lot along the way. With the help of many, I have finished previous races. Not always in first, and not always my best. However, I have retrained successfully and, in the process, put myself in the position to compete as a better trained performer. The proper preparation has given me the confidence to compete even better. Employing these strategies and tactics has provided me with opportunities for competing among other top performers.

The starter has fired the gun and I am off at a full sprint, baton in hand and making my way around the track towards you, the next runner. We're teammates in the same race but running different legs. I've given it all I have, and I'm rounding the corner to the final turn, baton in hand. You're waiting in the exchange zone eagerly. Awaiting the baton. But before you can run your leg of the race, you need the baton and a clean exchange to finish. Receive all my advice offered, and may you run with it and complete your leg of the race. Remember what I have told you in so many ways now, - don't ever drop the baton- manage your affairs, be disciplined and use all your resources. So, as you hear my footsteps approach you – listen for my command, "reach!" Start your sprint and feel the baton in your hand. Don't look back, you know what to do now. The baton exchange is flawless and in your capable hands. I have given you what I know to be true and authentic of how to be successful in college and beyond. It is tried and tested many times over.

Now it's your race to run, your race to win!

Don't drop the baton, sprint to the finish!

 Don't worry about the person next to you...

Just run *your* <u>*best*</u> race.

Continued Success!

References

Corkindale, G. Imposter Syndrome Managing Yourself Overcoming Imposter Syndrome. Harvard Business Review May 07, 2008.

Hoyt, E. (August 27, 2019). Student Life 20 Difference between High School and College Life. Retrieved From https://www.fastweb.com/student-life/articles/the-20-differences- between-high-school- college-life

National Student Clearinghouse Research Center. (Jun 27, 2018). First Year Persistence and Retention by Race and Ethnicity. Retrieved From https://nscresearchcenter.org/snapshotreport33-first-year-persistence-and-retention/

Perzynska, K. (June 6, 2018). Improve Presentation the Four Different Types of Learners – The Complete Guide. Retrieved From https://www.improvepresentation.com/blog/the- four different-types-of-learners

Sienkiewicz, T. (June 19, 2019). Why Flashcards Work. Retrieved From https://www.petersons.com/blog/why-flashcards-work/

Strive Academics. (June 7, 2017). How to Choose the Right Study Buddy. College and High School Study Tips. Retrieved From https://striveacademics.com/2017/06/07/how-to-choose-the-right-study-buddy/

Whelan, J. (May 8, 2019). Using the Leitner System to Improve Your Study. Retrieved From https://medium.com/@jessewhelan/using-the-leitner-system-to-improve-your-study- d5edafae7f0

About the Author

Reginald Ryder is a career higher education professional. As the youngest of five and a twin, he was raised in a USAF military family. His travels included stays in South Dakota, Georgia, Oregon, and Indiana.

As a first-generation student, he attended Ball State University and graduated with a Bachelor of Science degree in Political Science. After graduation, Reginald worked in the Admissions Offices at his alma mater and Butler University. He then moved to the Director of Multicultural Affairs at Allegheny College. Reginald also received his Master of Education in College Student Personnel Administration from James Madison University. Following graduate school, he worked at Cornell University in the College of Architecture, Art, and Planning as the Director of Multicultural Student Services. Reginald took a fork in the road and spent several years in K-12 as a Community Advocate, Assistant Dean, and Director of Guidance. His last 7 years have been in the field of education technology at 2U, serving as a MAT Placement Specialist and an Ed.D. Student Success Adviser in partnership with the Rossier School of Education at the University of Southern California. In 2018, he became an Adjunct Faculty member at Northern Virginia Community College teaching a College Student Success course SDV100. As a business owner of Thriving Life Coaching (TLC), he coaches individuals and college preparatory organizations to prepare students for the transitions that they will encounter in college.

<u>Passing the Baton - A Guide and Memoir of College Success</u> is an opportunity to learn of Reginald's tireless work as a mentor, coach and leader in guiding students from the admissions process to successful graduation. His work encompasses strategies for life-long learners up to doctorate level students. Reginald has effectively woven his candid story that took him from mediocrity in high school to influential positions, advanced degrees, and teaching students now how to master the transition to college life successfully. This pragmatic and insightful guide is from a rarely exposed point of view which is that of a student and seasoned retention specialist. This guide will help you achieve your greatness by applying what you learn from his strategies, so that you just don't survive the experience but academically thrive while preparing for your career and adulthood.

Reginald is a father of two kids, Kristina and Reginald II,. He has been married to Kim Amaker Ryder for 24 years. His family lives in the Greater Washington Metro area in Virginia.

Thriving Life Coaching – "Every student needs a little TLC."

Reginald Ryder is available to consult/speak with students or organizations contact via:

Website*: https://reginaldryder.wixsite.com/thrive*

Email: rryder4tlc@gmail.com

Instagram: @rryder4tlc

Twitter: @ReginaldRyder

Facebook: RRyder4TLC

LinkedIn: Reginald Ryder, M.Ed.

Made in the USA
Monee, IL
16 July 2020

36144640R00080